Stepping Beyond
Judgment

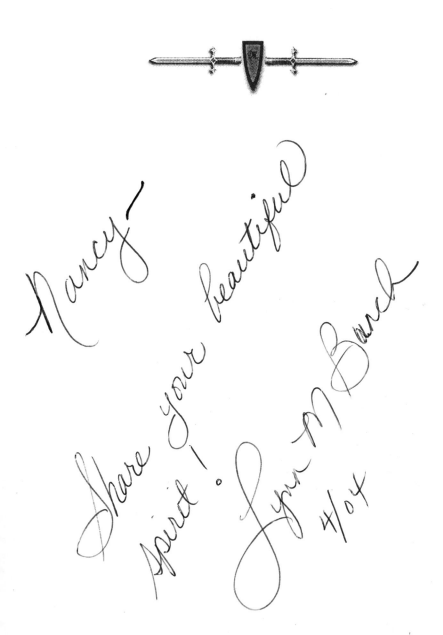

Nancy —

Share your beautiful
spirit!

Lynn M Barrick
4/04

Stepping Beyond
Judgment

Lynn M. Ferguson

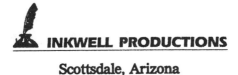

INKWELL PRODUCTIONS

Scottsdale, Arizona

First Printing, April 2001

Credits:
 Edited by Lisa Marie Berg
 Manuscript proofing by Jeffrey Steed and Laurel Cozzuli
 Typesetting/Design/Layout by Edgar W. Ball
 Karuna Designs & Services
 Cover design by Alexander Jenkins
 Printed in the United States of America
 Developed by Selfpublishersgroup.com

Published by
 Inkwell Productions
 3370 N. Hayden Rd., #123-276
 Scottsdale, AZ 85251
 Tel: (480) 315-9636
 Fax: (480) 315-9641
 Email: Specialty@Home.com
 Website: http://www.selfpublishersgroup.com

Contact above address to order any of Lynn's books or call/fax for more information.

Other Works By Lynn M. Ferguson:

 The Three Aspects Of Abundance Workshop
 Bridging The Gap: A Parent/Child Workshop
 Stepping Beyond Judgment Workshop

 For more information visit Lynn's web site at:
 http://www.intuitivedevelopment.org/

ISBN 0-9658158-9-7

Dedication

This book is dedicated to Archangel Michael. Thank you for your patience while awaiting my return.

Acknowledgements

My sons, Jacob and Adam for their commitment to me and sacrificing many hours of our family time. I am honored to be your mother.

Jeff, for supporting me when he found it difficult to do so.

My mom and dad for their commitment and love to each other, our family and the world.

My sister, Lisa, and our spiritual kinship. Thanks for keeping our dream alive.

Wayne, Boston and Marley for sharing their wife and mother.

My friends; they endured a lot of changes throughout the recent years and loved me through and through.

My clients; without them I would still be working at my day job – only dreaming of making a living doing what I love.

My publisher, Nick Ligidakis, for his unwavering spirit, loving motivation and continuous faith throughout this process.

My "Group;" without your consistent communication I wouldn't have been able to write this book: Edgar Ball, Cindy Bates, Lisa Berg, Patti Cranson, Marianne Greer, MaryAnn and George Hillman, Sandy Jenkins, Sandy Lahood, LuVerna Manuel, Darvina Nogales, Page McGee, Holly Sanchez, Jeffrey Steed and Carla Trujillo.

My thanks to all of the following people for their love and support in so many different ways: Amy Allen, Robert Bell, Pam and Jack DeGraff, the Ferguson Family, Becky Kistler, Janet Marracino, Tim McGinley, Agnes Newkirk, Grant Peurifoy, Holly and Carlos Sanchez, Ron Terry, Michael Ward, Patti Womack and Sherry Wray.

Contents

Preface

The intuitive work I have been doing on my life's journey is true to my heart. If there is anything that I may share with you in my writings that feels right to you, please put it to use in your own life's path, if for some reason it does not, leave it be. We are all very different and our differences must be celebrated. Our experiences are our own, never to be judged as wrong by ourselves or anyone else.

My desire in writing this book began with an empty heart that needed to be remembered. I have lived a great deal of my life for everyone else's approval, love, and acceptance. I have found in my quest for self-love that I am not alone. If at any level my story can reach someone else's heart and help them to remember themselves in a way that they have forgotten, my mission will be fulfilled.

I began this book by simply writing. I did not

know at the time that it would be a book, it was simply my way of expressing the teachings and dialogue I was having with my Guardian Angel. At some point in my writing I was told I would be sharing this with many others. Of course that scared me, as I am sure it would scare anyone. The exposure itself was enough to stop me right in my tracks.

When I was told I would be sharing myself on such a large scale the fear was immobilizing. I can honestly say I was following through with this divine plan, but not without protest. My mind could not let go of the fact that I was going to have to deal with a larger arena of people questioning my intent, integrity and, frankly, my sanity. This was not easy when I first began my business, and I was not looking forward to the scrutiny once again.

Exposure has always been my biggest fear. I had hurtled through a great deal of self-doubt and fear of appearing "different" in my private sessions, and my experience had been that as soon as clients were sitting with me in a session they had the benefit of seeing the whole picture. Meaning, I was this confident, loving, and very normal wife and mother that had simply embraced her gifts. Putting my life's experiences in writing was something altogether different. My reluctance, to say the least was HUGE! I can only say that the nudge, or should I say PUSH, to over-come that reluctance was ultimately bigger. Many of my writings are teachings that the angels have expressed through me and the rest are the experiences I have received in being connected to them.

I could not write this book without the incredible help I have received from everyone that has interacted with me in assisting my movement forward. There have been numerous people in my life that were instrumental in my growth, many who have no idea of their impact on my life, and many who do. I am forever thankful for their participation in my life's journey.

I am in no way finished with my journey of self-love. I hope to continue to find many different ways in which I may expand, express, and experience my human existence. For all who choose to read my writings I ask only that you begin with an open heart. My wish is that I touch your heart and help you on your movement to higher consciousness.

Prologue

  This book's intent is to allow all of us the ability to embrace a world of peace, harmony, and love, beyond anything we can remember. There was a time when we all experienced our hearts. The heart is where our connection to the non-physical realm is located. God, Universal Energy, or whatever Higher Source you may define for yourself, as well as the angelic and spirit realm, are all located in the heart. This has been forgotten for a great many years and we have become accustomed to believing that our minds are in control. This concept is not wrong, yet in the end, we will be left unfulfilled. The logic of the mind, or "logical mind," is a very important aspect of who we are, though the universe never intended it to be in control. My understanding is that if we transform our flow of Mind, Body, Spirit, to Spirit, Mind, Body, we will experience life's existence at greater levels.

  Many people have experienced communication

from the non-physical realm and made the transition to Spirit, Mind, Body, and many are still transitioning. This transition alone will bring about the shift in consciousness that is necessary for our planet to survive in a peaceful, loving existence. The truth is that communication with the non-physical realm will be the norm.

Judgment is the killer of Higher Consciousness. We fall into misalignment with God, or Higher Source, when we judge ourselves or others. I could stop writing now if only we could all get this one concept. I do not mean God is not present within us, I mean we literally move out of the alignment, or connection, with Higher Source. My intention in sharing my teachings through these writings are to allow others the vision I have been given, along with the tools to move smoothly from struggle, pain and fear, into divine wisdom.

I am in no way defining these teachings. They are not of any religious or specific belief system, they are simply tools for reaching beyond the judgments of your logical mind into the love of your heart and soul. My understanding of the world to come is amazing and the following pages are presented with the blessing that you, too, can enjoy the peace and love that is available in Stepping Beyond Judgment, and back into your heart.

Stepping Beyond Judgment

1

My Roots

My parents came here from Akron, Ohio in November of 1962 with their 3-month-old daughter, Lisa, my sister, in tow. My parents met in kindergarten class, started dating in high school and had a brief separation when Mom moved to Arizona during her junior year in high school. I believe it was during their exchange of letters that Dad realized he longed to move out west.

With minimal money, they courageously packed up themselves and their new baby and followed their hearts to Phoenix, Arizona – the land of cowboys and Indians. Both families balked at the idea, questioning their sanity. At that time people in the mid-west and back east had little knowledge of what the desert actually looked like and either pictured gunfights at the OK Corral or vast areas of nothing but sand. Undaunted, they made their dream a reality.

My story begins two and one-half years later, on January 26, 1965. The son my father wanted, or so I grew up believing, was not to be. My mother and father are both very devoted, loving parents. As with a lot of men, he longed for a son to carry on the family name and do the things guys do with sons. Everyone was sure I was a boy. So sure, in fact, that everything Mom received at my baby shower was done up in blue. Blue blankets, blue clothes, blue book; you get my drift. Imagine the surprise when out popped pink little me!

My father is one of those guys who lives and breathes cars. He's made his living in the automotive industry his entire life and although he owns and rides motorcycles, cars are his passion. On the day of my birth, Dad was in the waiting room when the doctor came out to give him the news of my arrival. As only car buffs can do, they ended up discussing the doctor's car until finally, Dad realized he didn't yet know of my arrival. The doctor informed him he was indeed the proud father of a six-pound baby girl. My father responded, "Great Doc, now about those tires."

It's a story that has been told frequently throughout my life, for its supposed humor, yet, each time it was told, the message I received was, "You were not wanted. I wanted a boy, not another girl."

My perception? My father wanted a son but, instead, got me. My judgment? He would have loved me more if I were a boy. Years later, and after many teachings, I pieced together how the *perceptions* and *judgments* of our stories, and the people in them, disrupt our connection with God.

The emotions that my feelings of being unwanted provoked were devastating. I felt alone and unworthy. Fortunately, through the love of my father and the love of myself, I now know that was never the truth. Indeed, it was only what I *perceived* to be the truth. Distinguishing perception from truth doesn't necessarily ease the pain of our experiences but, once understood, healing can begin.

I grew up in a middle class family home with three bedrooms and one bathroom. Boy, was that one bathroom difficult for my father! In living with three girls, getting his turn in the bathroom wasn't easy. Our house was very average. It was blue with white trim on the outside with two big evergreen trees in the front, a single Ocotillo cactus between them and, to the right of the yard, three aloe vera plants. All the neighborhood kids hung out in front of our house. We played many games there in the front yard at dusk, just as the sun was going down and the heat was subsiding. Typical games like Red Rover, Red Light-Green Light and Statues were our favorites.

Our house was always the favorite hangout throughout high school. In fact, it wasn't only kids who gravitated to us. I can remember my family waking up one morning and finding several of my dad's buddies from Akron in their sleeping bags on our *front* lawn. They made an impromptu trip to Arizona, arrived in the wee hours of the morning and camped out until we awoke to discover them. Our neighbors were either used to such odd comings and goings, or we were very well liked. Probably both. It wasn't our house that attracted people; it was our family. We've always been a very loving, hospitable and heartfelt family; all who entered our home felt the love present there.

One thing very unique about our house was the kitchen. My mom got an itch for something new and, to express herself, picked out her kitchen colors – Chinese red and hot pink. The brick wall was painted hot pink with a spattering of the bricks painted Chinese red, along with the side door and cabinets. You could see it beaming through the kitchen window if you were driving down the street at night. My mother joked that it was like a beacon calling to all who passed. She loved her kitchen, the beacon and all its brightness. Yet, I think the incessant teasing started to weigh on her. Later, she was forever asking my dad to repaint.

My dad was, and still is to this day, an insomniac. Since dad was always up throughout the night, he would paint or do some other creative endeavor that my mom had expressed a desire for and we'd awaken to new and exciting surroundings. We didn't have a lot of extras after the necessities, but re-painting always kept our house cheerful and bright. Living in my house was never dull.

My parents have been married for almost 40 years. To say I admire their marriage would not be completely honest. What I do admire about my parent's marriage is the true love that is at the core of their commitment to each other. They are an example of two people on a quest of remembering their spirit within the commitment of marriage. This has caused great pain and great amounts of growth for our family and I have learned much from both of them. They were an explosive combination at times. When they experienced hard times, the whole family experienced hard times. Mom could be both the detonator and peacemaker and Dad the TNT and fire extinguisher.

I can't tell you how many times my sister and I would be hauled out of bed, at all hours of the night and pre-dawn mornings to have a "family meeting." We would cringe whenever the light switch would be turned on knowing we were going to be tired come school the next morning. These meetings could last for hours and many times we couldn't recall the purpose for the meeting in the first place. I suppose when you're not able to sleep and are wide awake with something burning on your mind, it's hard to understand that others are not experiencing the same phenomena.

Dad's insomnia was both a curse and a blessing. The blessing is the impossibility of ever sneaking in after curfew, thereby, keeping us out of unnecessary trouble. Of course, we didn't quite see it that way back then. The good times were as wondrous as the hard times were intense. The support that they have given me throughout my life is, without a doubt, the most committed love for which I could ever ask.

When we come into this world, we believe that our parents are "God" in the female and male form. Life continues and, one day, we awaken to the realization that Mom and Dad are only human beings. For some, the awakening occurs very young. For others, this truth eludes them throughout life. At some point all that we have learned from these wonderful, honorable people is how to cope or not to cope in life. We see their different attributes and get to choose what we wish to further and what we wish to leave behind.

My father is compassionate, kind and loving. When there's an emergency he stays calm and level-headed – a man you want around in a crisis. He is a leader both in our family and in the community. He has always made sure that we never wanted for anything and instilled a sense of responsibility and respect for our family name and ourselves. My dad makes a difference in all he undertakes.

Dad has always been patriotic and wanted to be of service to his country. Since he had no war to join, he decided to serve his community. When I was about five years old my father joined the Phoenix Reserve Police Department. He did undercover work at night in "The Deuce," downtown Phoenix, which is not a pretty place to be after dark, and won the "Police Officer of the Year" award twice in a row. He was asked to leave the reserves and join the police force full-time. However, my dad refused saying that he chose to contribute his time, without pay, on the reserves to do his part in serving his country. I am proud to say that my dad served for eight years with an exemplary record.

It was toward the end that he started getting burned-out on the system and its machinations. He would put criminals in jail only to find them back out, sometimes within a matter of hours, laughing in his face. Feeling himself become hard and cold toward people and seeing how his attitude affected our family, he stepped down. Of course that didn't stop my dad from participating elsewhere.

Dad participated with our schools, getting to know the teachers and principals by name, working on different committees and even christening our neighborhood park. He was also a member of the Lion's Club and held a seat on the board of the Better Business Bureau. At one time, he owned a Texaco gas station, was a Service Advisor at a major Chevrolet Dealership.

He, then, started a company that developed courses for teaching women basic understanding of vehicle maintenance to protect them from being ripped off unnecessarily. The course was called "Under the Hood with Doug Lahood" and it went state-wide to the different Chevrolet dealerships.

Dad, then, started a family owned limousine company, La Limousine, where the whole family worked at one time or another. I, in my twenties, became General Manager for the last five years of the thirteen years we were in business.

Dad has always been a "hands-on" kind of guy and loves to work with his hands, literally. He welded metal sculptures and we went around the state to different art shows, seeing and meeting different people from all over the country. At home he painted a lot of portraits of our family and friends and encouraged us to try our hand at it too; though my sister and I preferred the "paint by number" kits. Presently, he is welding and sculpting originally designed candle holders as well as restoring various cars.

This is the dad I experienced throughout childhood and into adulthood and, as wonderful as he is, there is also the side of him that is explosive and combative. As a child, I rarely had direct experience with his temper, yet, I did experience the fall-out between him and my sister. Then again, what else could you expect when my sister was a smaller, female version of him (more about this later).

Then there was my mother. I had a quiet camaraderie with my mother that no one really understood which, quite frankly, angered my sister to no end. I spent a lot of time on my mother's lap as if giving and receiving energy all at the same time. We communicated with words, though more through our spirits. I knew that deep down she understood what my tea parties meant to me (the topic of Chapter Two) and encouraged them as much as she knew how to at the time. Mom was the quiet force of our family through which we couldn't have survived or thrived without, keeping the peace and keeping us all together.

It didn't exactly look like that from the outside because mom didn't say a lot, even when backed into a corner, but, when she did speak, we listened. She knew when to speak and when not to – when being silent said more than words. My dad was the parent who usually came to different events at school because of his flexible schedule but, if I ever needed Mom, all I ever had to do was say so and she would be there. It isn't the vivid recollections of anything in particular my mom did or said. It was simply the balance and peace within her that spoke volumes. My parents blended their parenting skills well and I can't imagine my life without either of them.

In addition to my parents and me inhabiting our home, there was also my sister. She and I shared a bedroom off and on, depending on who was visiting or living with us at the time. We spent the majority of our childhood in the same room until I was in seventh grade when we moved to a bigger house. Now, let me tell you what this was like for me. Lisa knew her position as the older sibling and felt as though I was born to serve her. She was the messiest person in the world and I was the cleanest – at least in my opinion. It was like Felix and Oscar all over again. In fact, that's what we were called.

My mom started working when I was in the

second grade, which left Lisa and I with a baby-sitter after school. Things were pretty equal with a baby-sitter to keep the peace. Then, when we got old enough to be home by ourselves, I became the slave – Lisa the master. If she wanted to watch something on television and I wanted something else, there was no contest. She was much more stubborn than I. There were certain rules of the house which weren't always followed, especially by Lisa.

We were not allowed to have people in the house while our parents were at work. Being two and a half years older, Lisa reached the "boy crazy" stage way before me. She and her friends would have their boyfriends over and they would be out on the back porch listening to music and smoking cigarettes. I began using my new found power of "If you don't let me..., I'm telling Mom and Dad...." The scale was becoming much more balanced in my favor; I had figured out the power of blackmail. Up until this point, she was definitely in charge.

My sister, I am convinced, was a gift from God. I can honestly say she is my very best friend in the world. Undeniably, this was not always the case. Our true friendship began after the birth of my first son, Jacob. Prior to that we were *sisters* and that is all. We shared the same parents, house, family pets, etc. However, there was nothing remotely close about us. If she liked chocolate, I liked vanilla and it didn't stop there.

Watching Lisa was like watching a movie and seeing cause and effect, directly and clearly. I can remember watching her interactions with our parents and consciously saying to myself, "Thank you for showing me what *not* to do and possibly saving my life in the process."

Through her experiences, Lisa showed me parts of myself I would not delve into deeply. In our early years of growing up she chose to learn the "hard way" or from so-called "negative" experiences. This is no longer true. The book, *Course in Miracles,* refers to our greatest teachers as "petty tyrants." Lisa was mine in my early childhood as well as that for many others.

Lisa is extremely strong willed and will allow no one to take that from her. What an inspiration! The contrary position, however, can and has been at times self-destructive to herself and to anyone opposing her. She was forever saying to me, "'Miss Perfect' doesn't do anything wrong." Why would I have to when the consequences were played out right before my eyes? I learned quickly "to not even go there." She didn't realize what a gift she was and at the time neither did I. She was, and still remains, a wonderful teacher for me.

When I said she's the side I would not delve deeply into, I am referring to the so-called "dark" side within each of us. She, on the other hand, was afraid to embrace the "light" side of herself. Even in our childhood, I can see how we balanced one another, only unconsciously. She and my father would get into a test of wills, trying to hold tightly to their own while breaking down the others. Lisa and Dad have a way of provoking one another by their mere presence alone and neither will back down from confrontation.

I remember an instance when I was about 15 years old and Lisa 17. We were standing in front of our laundry room door. She and my father were raging at one another. They are both very physical individuals and both were completely out of control – a nasty combination. I was begging her to apologize, to make it better, for whatever it was that got her there in the first place. However, I knew it wasn't going to happen. My dad took her head and pushed it into the door making a hole in it. Luckily, for Lisa, it was hollow and not solid oak. She refused to cry. She always refused to cry. I cried for her.

Lisa went through her childhood refusing to let my dad see her pain and I went through mine absorbing it for her. I shared my light with her in the only way she would allow me – feeling it for her. On the other hand, she embodied the injustice and rage that I kept bottled up inside, that part of me that was too afraid to speak for fear of the consequences and of being noticed. We have since worked diligently over the years at consciously embracing both sides of ourselves, forgiving the dark and empowering the light.

2

The Tea Party

One of my cherished childhood memories is of my tea parties. When I was around two or three years old, my Grandma Nema brought me a china tea set on one of her visits from Ohio. It was beautiful, dainty and elegant. It was white porcelain with yellow and gold flowers imprinted on the cups and saucers. Its beauty spoke to my heart. In my room was a small table and I would set it up impeccably with four place settings – for me and three of my friends. I would sit at that table for hours chatting with my friends – solving the world's problems. There were times when I would include our dog, Caesar, in our parties but, usually, it was just the four of us. People would come into my room and ask, "Lynny, who are you talking to?"

Eventually, I realized I was the only one that experienced my friends – the only one who knew they were sitting right there at my table. Many people called them imaginary but I knew there was nothing imaginary about them. They were as real to me as the family with whom I lived.

I would get lost in my tea party world for hours at a time until my sister or Mom would come into my room and interrupt me and I would abruptly stop talking to my friends. At the time, I had no clue that my guests were Archangels Michael, Gabrielle and Raphael. My mother would chuckle at how cute I looked and my sister would make fun of me in that condescending way that only she can do. I was astounded at being thought of as cute. I was having a very serious conversation with friends. My tea parties received a lot of attention from others. They would say, "Oh, look how cute she is sitting their with her make-believe friends – how intense she is."

I would think, "What are they talking about? I'm not talking to myself. Can't you see the other people here?" I saw nothing cute, unusual or "make believe" about my tea parties. They were as important to me as eating or breathing, an integral part of who I was in life – fulfilling me more than anything else. I enjoyed playing games with other children but it was the tea parties that nurtured my soul.

At first I didn't pay much attention to those on the outside looking in. In fact, I probably wasn't even aware that anyone else was present, other than my friends. Eventually, the teasing permeated my inner world and I became self-conscious about myself, my friends and the attention we attracted. I say "attracted" because everyone was drawn to watching me, especially my mother and sister, and, then, mimicking my mannerisms and words. Imitating me, they would crook their arm in my fashion and say, "Would you like some tea?"

Of course, I now know why. They wanted to be a part of the light that was radiating within us. They thought I was playing "pretend." I thought they were making fun of me. Although I have a very loving family, their poking fun at me was undoubtedly from ignorance and not deliberate attempts to hurt me. Nonetheless, at the age of five, I made a decision I was not going to be made fun of again. My tea parties were a thing of the past. My heart was closed.

Little did I know, in making that decision, I willed the angels and spirits to leave me alone – closing off my connection to that realm for many, many years. In the ensuing years, I felt isolated and alone, even when surrounded by people. My inner world was barren. Until, in complete desperation while standing in the shower, I called upon God to reveal Archangel Michael to me. One of my dear, dear friends would return.

3

Waking Up

My journey back to my heart started at the age of 25. I had been working at being a *better* person, by going to counseling, reading self help books, tapes, etc. However, the true quest for self-love and connection to a higher source did not pull at my heart until my second child, Adam, was born. After his birth, I was in a semi-numb state. I believed I had all a person could want – two beautiful children, a husband I loved, a nice home, vehicles and a well paying job.

My accomplishments seemed great compared to a lot of people, yet, something was missing – the fulfillment that these experiences were supposed to bring. My experiences weren't wrong and could have been completely fulfilling, except I felt a void within. I found myself living the life I *thought* would bring me happiness instead of what today I know does bring true happiness.

I began with small steps such as going to church, reading any self-help books I could get my hands on and forcing myself to become consciously aware of what was really going on in my life. It was no longer okay to ignore the hurtful words my husband was saying to me, that he wasn't coming home until late at night or that his drug use was running rampant. I continued a few more years hoping that I would be able to grow within my marriage. This was not the case. After seven years of marriage it was time to wake up.

One day I returned home because I had forgotten my checkbook; it's funny how God intervenes. I found my husband, Kevin and his friend doing lines of cocaine on our glass dining room table. Completely shocked and feeling betrayed at his total disregard for our family, I began screaming at him, "What if I would have sent one of the boys after my checkbook? Get your things and get out!"

He did leave. I'm sure his shame and relief of not having to hide his indiscretions motivated him as much as my insistence. This was the first step of a very messy battle that became gut wrenching, painful and, ultimately, a blessing for everyone.

I loved my husband with all my heart. We were high school sweethearts. Although that is loosely termed, because if you had seen the fights we had for three and a half years prior to our marriage, "sweethearts" would not be an accurate description. Should I have known better before marrying him? Yes. When you do not respect yourself, you do not expect anyone else to either. Neither one of us respected one another or ourselves.

We both experimented with drugs in and shortly after high school. When we married I was 20 and he was 22. I just assumed our experimental drug use was over. I didn't want to continue and took for granted that he felt the same. Unfortunately, what I considered "dabbling," he considered a way of life. It was a wedge so deep between us no counselor would give us a second look. We tried many – five to be exact. The love of our hearts was present. Yet, we were not making the same choices.

I am sure had I asked, prior to marriage, if he ever planned to quit smoking pot and other random drugs, he would have told me "no." It's ironic that we never ask the questions to which we already know the answers. I wasn't willing to ask. I desperately loved him and knew I would have to move on if I ever did find out the truth. The day I found him at the dining room table was my answer loud and clear.

From that day forward I loved my boys and

myself more. I knew I had to move on, no matter how much it hurt. Kevin left as I requested and we proceeded to go through many battles until our divorce was finally granted almost two years later. During those two years, like many others, I tried to reconcile my marriage for the sake of my boys as well as the dream I kept deep in my heart. Finding pictures of my soon-to-be ex-husband with another woman, nearly being strangled to death by him, having him point a loaded gun at me and that visit by the police ended any and all illusions of ever having the family my heart so desired. The battle scars were huge and very visible.

Our boys have remained balanced through the years due to the love and support they have received from Kevin's mother and grandmother along with the love of my family and God. Adam and Jacob are fabulous young men, now 10 and 13 years of age.

4

In Search of the Light

I dated a bit after my divorce and contemplated marriage again, to Brad – a man who was a long time friend of my sister's husband. Through this connection, he had also gained a friendship of sorts with Kevin. I loved this man and he me. However, Brad had a difficult time dealing with my first husband's hostility. This ultimately put too much of a strain on the relationship for it to survive.

After waiting for a call from him on Valentine's Day and receiving none, I felt an enormous let down. I will never forget that night. I called him in a last ditch effort to salvage what I already knew was unsalvageable. Yet, I still hoped for warmth and a sincere excuse for his having forgotten the day that is a celebration of the heart. What I received lacked all of the above.

I had done so much work on myself, having

actually made a list of what I needed in a relationship. I listed qualities and criteria I was willing to compromise on and those that were non-negotiable – a bottom line. I gave my list up to God and he sent me this very special relationship that met all of my heart's desires.

However, where I was willing to follow through with what was needed to fulfill my heart, Brad was unwilling to fulfill what his heart wanted. My heart was aching and, at last, I was clear it was time to move on and add another bottom-line to my wish list – a willing participant. God answered my prayers about three hours later with a phone call from Jeff.

When I heard the phone, I let the answering machine pick it up thinking it was my boyfriend but knowing it was over and that there was nothing more to say. When I heard Jeff's voice, however, I flew across my bed and grabbed the phone. I was shocked at my own reaction. What was I doing? I knew Jeff as an acquaintance and was dumbfounded at my reaction to dive for the phone. He wasn't even my type, or so I thought. When I asked him why he called now, at this time, on this date, he said, "I knew it was time."

I first met Jeff about a year prior to his call. I

knew there was a connection between us. In fact, I know that Michael directed the introduction because in that brief moment I had a knowing that he was the man I was going to marry. Now you might think I would have embraced this message and I probably would have. However, his physical resemblance to my first husband was enough to make my logical mind run in the opposite direction as fast as I could possibly go. I would run into him from time to time at friend's houses and gatherings throughout the year, never giving this connection much thought. So, you can imagine how surprised I was to be getting a call from him.

We remained on the phone until the wee hours of the morning sharing ourselves in a way that was truly beyond anything I had experienced with any man up to that point. He was able to understand the deep intuitive part of me that simply "knew" what people were feeling and I was fascinated with his ability to see colors around people when looking at them. Although, he did not know that they were called auras. It gave me the courage to look deeper into myself and ultimately find my truth once again.

When I look at the whole picture, I can see where Michael and God have always played a part in my life and in the synchronicity of it all. In my freshman year in high school, I had a classmate whose last name was Ferguson and I remember the impact it had on me. I was constantly drawn to the name and, yet, not because I neither liked nor disliked it. Even then, I knew there was something more to the name Ferguson and when Jeff told me his last name, the memory of years ago came present.

Jeff and I were married almost immediately without a bit of hesitation. We simply *knew* the time was right. We didn't try to articulate the "whys." We had helped bring out something in one another that had been closed off for many years. For me, that something was spirit.

Our families could not comprehend what possessed us to marry at the spur of the moment on April Fool's Day in Las Vegas, Nevada. To say they were shocked would be an understatement. Neither of us were prone to such spontaneous commitments–after all it took three and a half years of dating before I married the first time.

Our marriage began with a new home, cars, etc., as most everyone's does. However, we were sharing something I had never experienced before; nor had he. We didn't really give it a name (this experience) but I always knew it was God within me experiencing the fullness of marriage as I always dreamed it to be.

Jeff has never called his experience "God." It was simply for him "a quiet, peaceful sense from within" that he had always had and was now sharing with someone else. He has the ability to stay centered during good times and bad. This was very new to me as everyone I had experienced up to that point in my life were always quick to react when so called "bad" times were present.

As we moved along in marital bliss, we were also contending with my first husband and the battles that would spring up with him. Several people expressed their concern for my boys' welfare during their visits with their dad. Jeff and I were aware of his marijuana use. Yet, were trying to be fair and give him the benefit of the doubt – that he was being appropriate around them. We tried to convince ourselves that it was best for the boys to see their father no matter what. It was after my sister received an anonymous phone call that we changed our opinion as to his visitation rights.

The caller would not identify herself. She only said that she was the wife of someone who knew the boy's father very well and that they were in grave danger. Lisa listened to her and said that although she would pass the message on to me this was something that I had to hear for myself. The woman did not want to give her phone number but did agree to call me. I received a call and once again they wanted to remain anonymous. I told them I wasn't willing to honor their concerns for my boys if they weren't willing to honor mine with their names. We established trust with one another and I knew this to be a reliable source.

Jeff and I learned of the bigger picture that we didn't want to see and knew that the misuse of drugs was apparently overtaking Kevin's ability to see what was healthy for Jacob and Adam. This was horrifying for all the obvious reasons. The boys loved their father and I had to be the bad guy. After speaking with Jacob and Adam, Jeff and I found out details of neglect that they were feeling and the decision was made to cease the visitation until he made a commitment to the boys, their well being and his role as a father.

This decision did not come easy. Jeff and I knew we had to tell the boys everything that we had done in the past regarding our experimentation with drugs and the commitment we made in raising children. We strongly believed we could not expose their father's use of drugs without being completely honest about our own past use. Actually, Kevin's drug use was not exposed by us but revealed from his own negligence of keeping it away from them during visitations.

Neither Jeff nor I felt judgment toward him. We simply believed that he had lost perspective on the priorities in raising the boys. The commitment of raising children need not be clouded with drugs. Just as drinking and driving do not mix, neither so misusing drugs or alcohol and raising children. At this time I needed God badly.

5

Meeting Michael

I had been told on three separate occasions, over the course of several years, that my guardian angel's name was Archangel Michael. The first time I was reminded of Michael's presence was on a trip to Sedona, Arizona with my sister and her husband. At the time, I was separated from my first husband and not dealing well with the situation. So, they thought it would be good for me to get away.

We were wandering through the novelty shops in Sedona when we came across a lady reading Tarot cards. None of us believed or disbelieved in this sort of thing. In fact, we were all laughing at the absurdity of even having her read my cards. However, they encouraged me to give it a shot for the mere entertainment of it all.

To our surprise the woman was extremely accurate and told me many things that were true. She confirmed that I had been highly intuitive as a child and that I had chosen to shut it off because of my fears. She said that I was named after Archangel Michael, my middle name being Michelle, and that he was waiting for me. All I needed to do was ask for him to assist me and he would be there. I paid my money, took the tape with my reading and went on my way reminiscing from time to time on what she had said, but not giving it much thought.

The second incident was about a year later when my friend Robert mentioned having gone to see a woman whom he knew to have accurate psychic abilities. At this time, I wasn't consciously aware of multi-sensory beings, yet I knew I had a desire for something. I booked an appointment with this woman and she spoke to me of people in my life who had passed on, giving me their names and their messages. Along with the messages of those in my past, she told me I had Archangel Michael with me and all I need do was ask for his guidance.

On the third occasion, I found myself working with an intuitive counselor who mentioned the presence of an angel named Michael. She didn't elaborate, except to say that he is always with me. Each time I was told this, it meant nothing. I took nothing to heart.

This is at the point when the anonymous phone

calls and rumors were circulating about my ex-husband. A decision needed to be made. My logical mind was telling me how important it is for boys to be with their biological father. Although, my heart knew it was no longer safe for them to be around him.

Devastation, confusion and hysterical crying, while in the shower, is where I found myself when I finally asked God to reveal to me anything that would help, including this Archangel Michael that I had been hearing so much about. If he really was here to help me, then, now was the time. I could no longer do it on my own. I would like to say that calling upon God to reveal Michael was this huge dramatic scene with a divine light appearing in my shower stall, as the depiction I remember of Moses and the burning bush.

That was not the case. I am a knowing-based person which means I receive messages through an inner awareness. I didn't see, hear or feel his presence. I had an overwhelming awareness of his presence and I knew from that day forward that I was never going to be alone again. Michael's presence was as real as any person I could have touched. My life was forever changed. My tea party companion had returned.

The truth is, I never was without him. I was simply receiving his communication differently from when I was a little girl. Looking back, there were many occasions in which so-called unexplained coincidences saved me.

One very clear "coincidence" was when my ex-husband, Kevin, was completely irrational and very drugged out. He threw me to the ground, got on top of me and started strangling me. Just before I blacked out, I felt him being thrown off. Kevin then ran to the bedroom, got his nine-millimeter pistol, came back to where I was standing, having regained my composure, and he began waving it around while screaming at me. That's when the police came to the door.

After taking him into custody, the police officer told me they had received a call from our residence! An impossibility at best because Kevin and I were the only ones home and in the house. I suggested perhaps it was a neighbor who had made the call but the officer assured me that the call had been traced to our house and our number. Later, I would put together the strange unexplained occurrences of that day.

The next few days were intense. I filed for divorce and we went to trial for my husband's assault on me. I didn't want to prosecute. I just wanted the divorce. The state, on the other hand, wanted to prosecute.

It was at the trial that I learned about "hair-pin triggers." The slightest movement could set it off and apparently the gun Kevin was pointing at me not only had one; it was also cocked, loaded and ready to shoot. The state was using me as their only witness and wanted to know if I could tell them whether he had his finger on the trigger of the gun or the barrel? Apparently, this was the determining factor on whether or not they got a conviction. Honestly, I couldn't say and there was no conviction.

Oftentimes, I reflect upon upsetting occurrences, situations or coincidences that manifest in my life to seek out the hidden lessons or veiled truths. I realize now that not everyone does this. Days later, upon his release and much to my amazement, Kevin blamed me for his gun being confiscated by the police. His lack of responsibility and awareness that he could learn something positive from this event shocked me.

In that moment, I realized it was through Michael that Kevin had been pulled off me while I was being strangled. It was through Michael that the police were called and judging by the prosecutor's description of the fragility of a hair-pin trigger, it was also through Michael's intervention that the gun was kept from firing.

During that time of chaos, I remember experiencing calmness in my heart, never fear. It always seemed strange how safe I felt in the face of what could have been death. In retrospect, I know that what those three wise and wonderful women said was true. The presence of a "Michael," Archangel Michael, was always there forever at work in my life. All I had to do was ask. Fortunately, it didn't take my verbal acknowledgment of him to witness his presence. He was always there hearing my calls through my heart and not my words.

6

Michael's Impact

Now that I had established, in fact, that Michael's presence was with me and, better yet, always had been. You would think that life would show itself as Heaven on Earth. Oh, how I wish that were true! The trials and tribulations of establishing a communication with him were extremely difficult and revealed much about whom I thought myself to be as a person. I had to get to know me in a way that I never knew existed.

Of course, I asked the obvious question, "Why me?" He simply replied, "You were open and ready." At that time, our communication included no one. I had him all to myself and it felt incredible. I was sharing a bond that surpassed anything I would ever experienced in my life with anyone, even to this day.

The difficulty I had in the beginning was deciphering Michael's communication to me, as opposed to the self-talk of my logical mind. Michael helped me through this with various methods of awareness that were undeniably accurate and left no room for questions.

I was out to dinner with the family at a fast food restaurant when I was handed the receipt for our meal. I looked at the total and saw that it came to $16.16. At that moment Michael told me to remember those numbers. I made a mental note. Three days later, I received a letter from our mortgage company. We had sold our house a few months before and, in my mind, this letter could only be bad news. Much to my delight I found a refund check made out to us for $1,616.16! Instant shock set in, followed by jubilation at Michael's blatant display of how much he is a part of my life.

On the other hand, however, there was Jeff's skepticism of Michael's presence in my life and the belief as to whether he indeed existed – let alone accepting whether messages I was receiving from him were true. Coincidence was Jeff's diagnosis. I was confronted by his lack of faith. After all, he seemed to have known and trusted my words and experiences when we were first together. Then again, my knowing certain things at that time was labeled "gut instinct" or "intuition;" something Jeff could handle. Once I knew and acknowledged the name Archangel Michael as the source behind my intuitive gifts, the dynamics of our relationship definitely shifted. Jeff asked me to call our mortgage company to verify that the check was real. The woman at the mortgage company also expressed how unusual the amount of the check was. Yet, after double checking the figure, she verified its accuracy.

To this day I find myself in awe of the messages that the angels bring me. The only difference between my perspective and that of others is the fact that I no longer question their authenticity. There was a time when we all trusted what we knew to be our own truth. As children, our spirits were so a part of God that we didn't find it strange to see His miracles all around us. It was when we became aware of our human reality and it's logic, that we also became dense and skeptical of God's little miracles.

I too remember a time at the beginning of my intuitive counseling when I lost sight of God's miracles. I was getting a lot of flack from non-believers for my communication with Michael, other angels and people who had passed over. People chose to ridicule what they did not understand instead of experiencing me and my work. The weight of their accusations was daunting. However, I continued the pursuit of my work and the challenges that accompanied it. I was beginning to feel very discouraged. Michael, to boost my morale, would ring my phone every night before I went to sleep. Amazingly, it was never at the same time since I would go to bed anywhere between 9:30 and midnight. It was just a quick "ring...ring," signaling to me that I was doing a good job and should not get discouraged.

I was also communicating with other angels and spirits. The feeling was like a vibration coming from inside my body. It was very intense–especially when I was dreaming. I felt a "thickness" around me, what I now know to be my etheric body. At the time, these experiences were very strange and frightening. I would see shadows of the angels and spirits or small particle-like objects flashing and moving about.

In this transitional state, I was fully aware of the etheric reality, yet, always focused on the physical/human realm in which I was grounded. Whenever someone interrupted me, as in my tea party sessions, it would jolt me out of the experience and I would feel very exposed, vulnerable and hypersensitive to my surroundings.

Most individuals experience the etheric realm while in their sleep. My first recollection of spending time in that reality was around the ages of five to seven. I would be deep into a dream or etheric state and would awaken to my parents calling my name and finding myself in the bedroom closet crying. I recall only the red painted shelves in my closet, the left over Chinese red from our kitchen, and the feeling of being lost. One episode, as my sister tells it, was when I pretty much went into hysterics, scaring her so badly that she thought I was never going to come out of this "state." Lisa had heard somewhere to *never* wake a sleepwalker for they could die of a heart attack.

So, there she stood at the door of our closet whispering my name, praying I'd snap out of it. I did, eventually, and proceeded back to bed as if nothing happened. Lisa's fear impacted me so greatly that my dreams no longer resulted in sleepwalking. It was fear I was feeling, while being awakened, that made me cry – not knowing where I was, as in the closet, or why I was there. I was receiving messages in my dream state and since I didn't know what they were and there wasn't anyone who could explain what was happening to me, I became fearful.

I remember, as a child, asking my parents to explain the dreams, the vibrations, the flashes of light I experienced and their frustration at not knowing how to answer me. Michael said their inability to remember their own experiences of childhood resulted in frustration and perceived inadequacies as parents. Michael has since helped me to heal my fears and memories of the past for which I am grateful. Had these healings not taken place, I would not have been able to help my son through similar experiences.

I recall my youngest son, Adam, a visual intuit (meaning he receives his messages through visual images), coming to me in the middle of the night in a frightened state or with more of a frozen stare. He was clearly seeing something that I wasn't seeing and talking with me, though not conscious of me. He was frightened by the "things" he was seeing–something he couldn't describe.

The truth is I was scared! My faith in Michael was strong, yet, up to this point, I had been dealing with *my* experiences and beliefs outside this physical realm. I had to let go of my fear and align myself with Michael. Once I centered myself, I was able to ask and receive a message from him as to what I needed to do.

Before bedtime that same evening our family had been having a wonderful time playing with balloons in the living room. We were throwing them into the air seeing if we could keep them up off the ground. The "things" Adam was seeing were little "light beings" that wanted only to continue to play with him after he had gone to bed. My first responsibility was to let go of my fear, realign with my truth, see the situation for what it truly was and help Adam through it so he could alleviate his fears and find his own truth. It turned out to be an uncomplicated process of simply and gently calling him back to this earthly reality.

I believe each generation takes their memories and beliefs of God to the next higher level than the generation that preceded them. I had done so much work on clearing away old wounds by this time that it was much easier for me to help Adam than it had been for my own parents to help me.

7

Eye of the Storm

There is only one thing that stands in the way of knowing, feeling or sensing our connection to God. It is our strong right and wrong judgment that we direct toward others and ourselves. If we could stop the doubting process that throws us out of this divine connection, we would need nothing else. Most of us spend our waking hours trying to connect to people, situations or things that we believe, on some level, will help us feel the peace, harmony and contentment of heart.

The truth is that any connection to something other than God is a momentary "fix" usually lasting only until the next crisis or, metaphorically speaking, until the next two-by-four to the head or tornado impacts our lives and throws us into panic and fear. The solution is to ask for guidance when we feel ourselves combating outside forces and stop giving them more validity than the inner peace that God provides.

Gratefully, I drew upon this guidance while living with my parents and was given a valuable lesson that Kevin provided so generously. One afternoon, Jeff came to take us to dinner and as the boys waited for us in the front yard, Kevin and his new wife drove by on his Harley Davidson. Upon seeing the boys alone, they decided to pull up in front of the house to speak with them.

By this time, the boys had witnessed enough incidents of abuse that they did not welcome the possibility of interacting with their father's hostility again. So, when Kevin called Jacob over, Jacob stood frozen in his tracks.

It was at this moment that I walked out to see a mixture of love and confusion on his face as Kevin started walking toward him. I stepped in, asking Jacob to step back and attempted to speak to Kevin with the hopes of diffusing any confrontation. I explained that the boys needed continuity and that if he wanted to begin seeing them again, we would need to go through the court system. He called me a few choice names, gathered a large amount of spit into his mouth and spat it directly onto my face and hair. Then, he took off just as Jeff and my father walked out of the house.

I was mortified, humiliated and frankly downright shocked at what he had done. The man I had married just out of high school was no longer behind the eyes of the man that spit in my face. There wasn't a trace of him left that I could see. At first, I was furious. After all, despite the years of trying to work things out with him and turning the other cheek when he didn't pay his child support or keep his obligations to the boys, he was still hostile and vengeful toward me – continuing to blame me for his shortcomings.

In the years after we divorced, Kevin got backed up on his child support payments owing $5,900.00. I made a phone call and he was picked up and put into jail for a few days until he was able to borrow the money for his release. I didn't like the fact that it was the result of my call that he was there. However, I also had to support my children.

It definitely wasn't good between us. But, somewhere along the way, we managed to become civil and when he again got behind on his payments, we made a court date. I picked him up and, once we were in front of the judge, I asked that the now $6,700.00 due the boys be forgiven, his child support reduced and that he be given another chance. The judge made me repeat, then and there, that I understood in forgiving the past amount, I could not, in the future, go after it. It was completely erased from the records as delinquent and owed. I acknowledged that I did, indeed, understand. Kevin and I went to lunch after court that day and I felt we both found a remembered memory of why we had married so many years before.

Unfortunately, I had forgotten all the negative energy churning inside of him and that I had always been the safest target to release on. Had I remembered that, his treatment of me in front of my parent's house would not have been so surprising! When I finally calmed down, I asked Michael what that was all about? He told me, "When you get too close to a lion that hasn't been fed, he will strike out." I, then, understood some of what he was going through. He had not had the best childhood and had never healed the wounds from his own relationship with his father. Therefore, he had no idea what to do for his own children.

Although this did not mean I was going to subject my children to any more of his destructive behavior, I did come to a place where my love for his soul had been regained. I felt empathy for his wounded spirit in a way I had never before experienced. No longer did I judge why he wasn't the father we wanted him to be. He simply wasn't yet willing to heal himself.

The "lion" Michael was referring to, that hadn't been fed, was his soul. He was still abusing drugs, trying to survive, and his spirit was void of self-love. No one could give him love because he did not love himself. It reaffirmed that my boys and I could not be in physical contact with him nor could we, or would we, condemn or judge him. We would love his soul forever – praying that someday he would awaken to his true God Self.

This was a valuable lesson. Yet, teaching my children to love his soul as well as helping them to understand their own boundaries, was not an easy task. God, giving them a wonderful dad in Jeff to physically love them and be there for them in ways their biological father couldn't, does not take away the love they feel for Kevin nor the love he feels for them. My boys are extraordinary young men. The work they have done for themselves and the spiritual beings that they show themselves to be every single day is very honorable. They have dealt with a lot of turmoil in their young lives and have become stronger for it.

Also, I saw in Jeff a calmness that wasn't always present in my life. I have never met a man that can stay centered in the midst of his wife going through such turmoil and not get angry or want restitution. It was a gift watching him stay centered in the bad times – always knowing what to do without letting his ego take over and rule the kingdom of hatred. He is a magnificent teacher for me of self-love. The stability of his soul cannot be shaken by worldly affairs.

This incident impacted upon me and also effected my interactions with family and clients. We are all the richer for the experience. The challenges I was given in dealing with my ex-husband gave me the ability to step beyond judgment that, in the past, had seemed justifiable. Kevin gave me many reasons to feel justified in being right and in judging his behavior. Yet, God gave me wisdom that has far exceeded any rationale to condemn him.

8

Who Are We?

In the beginning of our spiritual journey we experience difficulty in remembering how to connect to God. Once our memory is jogged, connection becomes second nature. Finally, toward the end of our quest of learning, we remember "who we are" as a Divine Connection to God Eternal and can, therefore, have difficulty staying connected or grounded in the reality of human consciousness. Human consciousness seems chaotic and our natural response is to lift out of its reality. This sometimes feels as though you are losing touch with reality or going "insane." Some people at this last stage of remembering "who we are" actually give up and become ungrounded. I experienced this pull within myself.

My best conversations with Michael occur in the early morning hours when I first awaken for the new day. I lay in bed with my eyes closed and converse anywhere from 15 minutes to a couple of hours, depending on what Michael has to impart to me for that day. I cherish this time.

On one occasion, I had been having a challenging week, nothing specific, just challenging. One morning, I awoke to darkness. Not only was the room dark, my soul felt darkness. I thought Satan had taken me over which seems a very insane thought as I don't actually believe Satan is anything more than our own darkness or negative thoughts.

All of a sudden it was real! I thought for a brief moment, "Maybe Matt (more about him later) was right; maybe I am Satan!"

I lay in bed stricken with morose thoughts of my death, of nothingness and of slipping into an insanity from which I would never return. I was paralyzed with fear. I reached for the phone and called my sister who, luckily for me, lived next door. Lisa came over and sat on my bed holding my foot. She didn't say anything profound. She just sat with me – helping me to balance and ground.

Thankfully, I got through it. It was then that I realized that once you make the choice to stay and serve God on this human level, *you are given the tools to keep focused and in alignment.* As I said, thankfully, I got through it; many choose not to.

When you are clear with "who you are," you must, at that point, choose, as Jesus once said, "to be in the world but not of it." This choice seems to be a simple one. However, when you are the one making it, it is not so easy. The world does not really offer a great deal to those who have reached this point, except to be of service to God. This is not always pleasant for it poses a challenge of staying centered and not getting sucked into the human drama.

It is very important to mention that the choice is always ours to either stand in the "eye of the hurricane" where it's calm or remain in the chaos. God gave us this right by giving us free will to choose him or not to choose him.

Remember, there is no right or wrong because we are only here to learn from our life experiences so as to remember "who we are" and, undoubtedly, "who we are" is the part which feels the most difficult. Remembering that no matter what judgments we make upon others or ourselves, we cannot, in the long run, forget "who we are."

There is always a part of us that does not understand exactly what is necessary to move us forward. Yet, if you continue to reconnect yourself to God, there will always be the truth on the other side of our struggles in life. Remain open for all experiences to give you the entire truth and allow yourself to experience the fullness of what God has for you.

This can sometimes feel very disconcerting, especially if we are standing in the way of our own abundance from God. We always have the ability to step aside and receive the goodness from God. However, most of us don't believe it can be that simple.

Now let's speak of the mistake that many of us make in thinking that "what we do" is "who we are." This is far, far from the truth. Yet, it is a form of mistaken identity that we must all go through before fully understood. "Who we are" is the gas station attendant, the business owner or the preacher who understands that what he or she does to earn a living is not who he or she is. We experience the peace, love and joy coming from him or her every time we come in contact with that person.

Adversely, we have also experienced the gas station attendant, the business owner, the preacher who thinks that what he or she does *is* who he or she is and we experience judgment, lack of joy, non-fulfillment and ego instead. "Who we are" is a divine connection to God and remembering that divine connection is only a matter of *when.*

We *will* find our way and once we get to this level, begin the process of determining what would be the most beneficial service to God, yourself and others in the most expansive way possible. Most likely, you will go through many tests to determine what His will looks like and, in the process, weed out many things you thought were your "gifts" to impart to the world. Also, you may find many that were just the road to getting you there. It matters not what you do with who you are as long as it serves God, yourself and others in the greatest possible way.

Some people think it must be something of a high spiritual status in order to serve God. For God, it matters not what we do; only that we stay grounded in who we are while we are doing it. This is the trick–to stay centered while the world's human consciousness tries to pull you out. There isn't anything wrong with human consciousness; going in and out is normal. It's getting stuck there that causes the disharmony.

Serving God is a remarkable experience whether you are caring for children, running a nation, bagging groceries or helping people on their spiritual journey as I have been guided and have chosen to do. Once you know "who you are," what you do with that will simply be the greatest expansion of God for *you.*

9

The Gift of Detachment

In returning to our heart connection we will process through many past memories, experiences and lessons – whatever is needed to get there. We need to allow ourselves the freedom to know that we all get thrown off course from time to time and sucked into our human consciousness, our logical mind. This is not "bad." We merely need to ask the question, "Does it serve me?" Staying centered consists of continuously being *aware* of what is happening within your inner self and asking yourself if you are experiencing "the calm."

Understand, this calm, to which I refer, isn't necessarily a "feel good" kind of place. In the midst of life's madness, we all have felt a certain calm that we sometimes may have experienced as happiness, discomfort or, even, sadness. Yet, always present was peace, tranquillity or "calm" and we knew, without fail, in what direction to proceed to move forward in our life.

Early on, while still working full time and, then, only contemplating doing intuitive counseling as a profession, my niece Marley became very ill with a temperature of 103 degrees. At the time, Marley was only seven months old. She was burning with a fever, yet, very coherent and even happy, as though nothing was amiss.

Normally, any mother would call a doctor first thing if her child had such a fever, yet, Lisa got the message to call me and work through whatever was causing her illness. I got the message that Marley didn't need to go to the doctor. She was clearing away impurities within and she would be fine with a cool bath. Lisa bathed her and Marley cooled down for about an hour or so. Then, Lisa called again saying her temperature was now at 105.

I again asked what needed to be done and Michael told me that Lisa needed to take her outside in the fresh air, rub her down with ice and pull the energy from her. All the while I was relaying this message, my logical mind kept getting in the way saying, "But, maybe you should take her in to the doctor, too." After all, this was my sweet little niece and I didn't want to be wrong and have anything happen to her.

Lisa stayed centered throughout telling me that she trusted my messages and that, when and if a time came that she knew to take her to the doctor, she would do so. She took Marley outside, gave her a rub down and pulled out the energy. Within 20 minutes, Marley's temperature was back to normal. Lisa and I stayed in the "calm," even though it didn't feel "good" and we detached ourselves from the fears of the circumstances connected to her daughter.

Do I give this message to anyone calling me for medical input? No. I listen to my message and then pass it along. It is the responsibility of those coming to me, to discern for themselves what to do with the messages. Lisa's confidence in my intuitive abilities, as well as her own, moved us through the attachment to what stops us on an intellectual level and into our connection with God and the miracles that are wrought through trusting God within us.

Occasionally, I would stop myself from going forward with this work out of fear of what might happen if I gave someone a message and something terrible happened. Michael reminded me of a time when I had to meet with Jacob's teacher and was told that he should go on Ritalin to help him with his school studies.

I neither condemn nor condone taking medication. Rather, I knew, as Jacob and I had discussed previously, that this was not the route he wanted to take. Jacob said that he wanted to get good grades but he didn't want the effect that the medication would have on his life, outside of bettering his school grades.

We sat down and discussed what it would take for him to make good grades and made a plan of organization at home as well as at school, such as setting him up with tutoring, etc. We took responsibility for the message the teacher had given us about the medication and used our own discernment as to what to do with it.

When it was conference time, again, I met with his teachers and every one of them commended both Jacob and I on our commitment to his schooling. He was making the same passing marks without medication as students that were on medication. The teacher was responsible in relaying his message about the medication. I was responsible in my response to it.

The occasional doubts about something terrible happening to my clients no longer exist. Michael reminded me that my only responsibility is staying in alignment – receiving and relaying accurate messages without adding my own interpretations. This is where a lot of people tend to foul themselves up, by making their own interpretations as opposed to keeping it clear and concise. The "calm" is the centered connection to our God Consciousness.

Unfortunately, most of us act with a human consciousness that drives us to remain *attached* to our human emotions, feelings and actions. My intent is not to refer to our human consciousness as bad in any way, but only to point out that it serves as a connection to the earth plane and to other individuals on a physical level.

Attachment is the thing that throws us into judgment of others and ourselves. When we get attached to someone, something or some situation, we begin the process of falling out of connection with God; it takes us out of our "center." Although, I now find a certain amusement when I see my attachments pop up. That hasn't always been the case.

My husband took me to an expensive steak house for my 32nd birthday. While I was enjoying my filet mignon (I love filet mignon), I got a message from Michael, loud and clear, to enjoy my steak because, after this meal, I would become a vegetarian. Needless to say, my instant reaction to this was, "I don't think so!"

Adamantly, I dug my heels in and wanted to know why? His reply was simple. I needed to lighten the vibration of my energy in order to handle the intense work for which I was about to embark. Readily, I admit that my attitude with Michael has been one of "Do I have to?" which is much like that of small children pleading with their parents not to make them do their homework even though they know it will bring good grades.

Knowing Michael would never request anything that was not necessary for my spiritual growth and well being, I listened and followed through with his message. At that time, I assumed that my vegetarian status was forever. Fortunately for me, as abruptly as he came to me with the message to quit eating meat, he also came to me 18 months later with the message that I could integrate meat back into my diet with poultry and fish first, then, if I desired, meat.

Was he kidding? Of course I desired. In making the choice to detach from my perceived agony of what his request would cost me, I found that following his direction was easier than I could imagine when not engaged in my drama.

Attachment comes in all forms. Many challenges came to me through relationships with friends and family. My commitment to the integrity of my chosen work calls for me to be brutally honest sometimes and several close friendships have suffered because of it. Most of my friendships from the past contained a lot of what I call "fluff." I define "fluff" as conversations filled with what sounds nice, what we want to hear, avoiding subjects that bring pain or sadness and deflecting truth which could move us forward. Fluff is neither good nor bad. It is just something I found I had to dispense with so I could start speaking *my* truth.

I came to understand that the mere stuffing of emotions causes us to put unnecessary amounts of energy into being non-authentic. I can sense when something is out of alignment just by being present with people. The honesty I bring into my relationships, whether with family or friends, I ask for in return. It may not always be easy or fun to be in a relationship with me. However, the dedication it brings to our lives is rewarding.

For many years, especially during my high school years, I chose to shut down this part of my intuition so I could hold back any comments that might be confronting to people and cause them to dislike me. The amount of energy it took to stop myself from speaking what was in my heart was enormous and, in doing so, I stored it in my logical mind resulting in judgment on myself. So many times I consciously remained silent choosing to say nothing and having a superficial relationship with friends as opposed to speaking my truth all for fear of losing friendship.

When I began to look at my own life and the

issues in it, I realized that replaying all my stories of pain and hurt no longer served me and I would have to go deep to heal them. The same became true for me in my friendships. Friends came to me for advice, rehashing old wounds time and again, wanting my help and yet shutting down when I gave it.

It came to the point when I had to let some of them go. I didn't want to hurt them with truths about issues I could see while they were unwilling to see them. I chose to release these friendships rather than shut myself down. Many friends thought I was judging them and the attachment I felt of no longer physically having them in my life was a price I was willing to pay in order to be true to myself.

I knew our hearts shared love for the past, present and future, whether our paths ever crossed again. After some time, those willing to look deeper understood that I was simply pointing out a wound that needed attention so they could heal it and step fully into their heart. Those friendships have become stronger.

Friends were not the only people I had to release. I also had clients who believed my discernment was judgment. Michael's energy is quite intense and the bluntness in which it is sometimes delivered does not always work for them. I begin my relationships, whether it be client, friendship or family, by letting them know that the method in which I align with Michael is one of climbing straight up the mountain as opposed to going at a gradual ascent around the mountain. Neither method is right or wrong. It is simply the way my energy with Michael is used.

For many years people have said to me, "You are so intense," and I would cringe as if I had just been called a horrible name. I have detached the emotions that I had tied to the word "intense" and, now, embrace the fact that this is the way I am – no more excuses. Michael's energy is intense, hence my intensity. As I said, my work with Michael does not work for everyone. Letting go of people that choose a different path, however difficult, is essential if I am to remain authentic to God and myself.

When we are born, we live completely in our heart space until we are taught logic. Unfortunately, most of us go from connecting to our heart to connecting to our logic or ego instead of learning to balance the two. Many of us have been living in our logical mind in order to survive childhood wounds and circumstances. We do not comprehend that with the mind, or logic, come emotions.

We think that emotion is a function of the heart and, therefore, do not proceed with the messages we are given by God and our guides for fear of the pain. Our mind is what connects emotions to our memories of the past. Our heart is what is connected to God and God is here to help us remember Him, not to harm us to the point of forgetfulness.

Attachment can also come in the form of detachment. To become completely detached from the world can also be detrimental. I spoke of the incident in which Kevin spat in my face and then took off upon seeing Jeff and my father. I remember thinking how wonderful it was that I had a husband that didn't react to his hatred and, in fact, I am fortunate to have had that.

However, what I realized later was the extent to which he didn't react. Emotions run very high in my family whether it is happiness, sadness, grief or anger and especially anger. When expressed, it is expressed very passionately. When expressed in the negative, it can be very frightening and when expressed positively, it is jubilant.

My father is half-Lebanese and half-Irish – two very passionate cultures. They show up both positively and negatively. My father's first instinct is to avenge the family name. So, you can imagine how protective he became when he found out Kevin had spit in my face. Jeff, on the other hand, stayed very calm throughout the telling of the whole ordeal. Like

I said, I was thankful it didn't get volatile and we were able to deal with the matter appropriately through the court system.

Later, I realized the degree to which Jeff was emotionally unaffected. I wasn't looking for him to go after my ex-husband with a baseball bat. Yet, there was an absence of empathy or compassion for what his wife and sons had just experienced. There seemed to be no depth of concern in his communication with others and myself about it. Jeff had detached from expressing all emotion. Given the background I had come from, this response, which at first seemed refreshing, only later revealed his unwillingness to relate.

10
Evil or Darkness

I do not believe there is anything that possesses a power greater than God. Thus, believing that something other than God has any power over us does not exist. That is not to say that so-called evil or dark energy does not exist. It merely does not have any power over Light or God. When you live this concept, you will no longer believe in darkness or evil forces. You will merely stand in the Light and the darkness will cease to be.

This negative energy has many names: Satan, darkness, the devil, evil, etc. Whatever label you use, it has absolutely no power over God, Universal Energy or Light. I refer to this negative energy as "lower level consciousness." Many people live in various degrees of consciousness from the extreme lows to the enlightened highs. We are the ones that give this energy the power by acknowledging it as real. I am not saying it is not there nor very real to some people. However, when it is given energy on any level by fearing it, then, it regains power in your life.

When working with clients, I simply acknowledge the energy it's being given and put my full attention on God and Light. When people are living in this lower level consciousness, I refer to this as Hell on Earth. Fear, in and of itself, is a precursor to this state of living. Individuals experiencing fear are not experiencing the presence of God. The Universe is always waiting for us to connect or align ourselves. Yet, our ability to exercise our right to free will sometimes throws us out of that alignment.

God is the one power. Therefore, anything opposing God falls into the category of fear. I am not referring to the fear we experience before doing something that we "know" is divinely guided such as jumping off of a high dive to face your fear of heights. The fear I am referring to is the one that literally separates you from God. You know the difference because one will give you an anxious or exciting feeling while continuing to stand in the "calm" place in your heart. The other will cause great questioning and doubt for everything that comes your way into the deepest aspects of yourself.

I had a situation when I needed to face my

own truth about "good and evil" early on in my work. I had been working pretty steadily with a client, Chad, on transforming his dark energy into light. He is extremely intuitive, yet, could get swallowed up in his "darkness" or the aspects of himself he feared looking at prior to our sessions.

He likes to express himself through his body art, kick boxing and karate. Though I can appreciate this form of expression, Chad's intentions or reasons would bring energy that wasn't always in his highest good. Sparring must be done with the correct intentions of the heart. Otherwise, it simply becomes an outlet for aggressive unresolved issues to emerge. We had worked through clearing many of his old issues that were out of alignment with his heart and resolved much of the anger that laid deep within him, so much so that we weren't having sessions as regularly.

He returned to me quite some time later, with this black cloud hovering above him. He had fallen out of alignment and the "demons," as he referred to them, were running rampant around him once again. The continued dedication to looking deep within himself and working diligently on his alignment with God was essential to his living peacefully. He had not been doing this. He informed me that he had been to see a Shaman to help him release these so-called "demons" and the Shaman had sent him away.

My first reaction was also to send him away. After all, if a Shaman feared his energy, who was I to think I could help him. I asked Michael if there was anything I could do to help. The answer was "yes." He explained to me that what the Shaman did in sending Chad away was the right thing for him to do as their culture believes as much in the dark as in the light and learns many great lessons from both. Being that *my* truth, or belief system, holds power only for the light, I was able to dispel the "demons" or darkness which Chad had come in contact with and he was able to once again hold his own light. I had to conquer my own logical fears of doubt that the darkness had any power over me.

Another time I had been working with a client, Matt, for several months. We met while working at the same company. I was doing intuitive work–only part-time. I didn't know Matt on a personal level at all when Michael told me to go to him with a message. I didn't want to. I shared myself and my connection to Michael with a lot of people who knew me and with whom I had some kind of credibility. However, exposing myself to a virtual stranger was more than I was willing to do.

Eventually, Michael's persistence won out and, as frightening as it was, I gave him the message and we ended up talking for over an hour. When I left the company to do intuitive counseling full-time, Matt became a client. I came to honor this man, his position in management at the company and his position at his church. Although his church did not believe in speaking with people who had passed on (angels and the like), Matt knew my connection to Michael to be true as well as the connection he was experiencing with his guide. Matt and I both learned and grew a lot out of our sessions.

Approximately eight months later and after a number of sessions, Matt showed up for an appointment. Much to my surprise it was a Matt I didn't know. The Matt that showed up was a Matt of the mind and not of the heart. He had come to the path in his journey of remembering who he was, when, the ego or human consciousness stepped in and tried to erase his memory of the path that led to God.

Matt was so full of fear. He accused me of following Satan! I was devastated. I felt betrayed by his about face – his lack of trust that would actually have him thinking I was following the devil! I felt myself losing center–giving him my power. I then remembered Michael was with me and I allowed him to bring me through it.

Matt was so close to his truth and although I

knew that he could live in *his* truth and in the truth of his church, even though they appeared contrary, Matt did not and made it about me. At that point in the session Matt and I could have ended it in being at odds with each other. We did not. I stayed in my center and he again found his heart. That turned out to be Matt's last session and, as uncomfortable as it was, we completed our time together with love in our hearts and respect for each other's truths.

I have found that in embracing both sides of God, be it darkness or light, we will all at some point have to deal with the parts of us that we believe are something evil or bad. This was my test. I found myself much stronger from these experiences. However, while dealing with them, it, of course, seemed more of a challenge than I bargained for. Michael did not agree. It goes back to that old adage that God never gives you more than you can handle.

11

Judgment Vs. Discernment

Discernment is a very tricky word. The dictionary defines it as, "The quality of being able to grasp and comprehend what is obscure; to detect with the eyes or senses; to understand the difference." I use this ability very much in my work. In fact it is imperative for me to have this ability in order to help those with whom I am working. Many people tend to misinterpret this ability as judgment. Discernment resembles judgment in certain situations. However, the differences between them are very distinct.

Using discernment is what gives me the ability to detect whether someone is in the "hurricane" or the "eye of the hurricane." This is extremely important in order to "know" exactly how to proceed with the session or interaction with a person. If the person I am working or interacting with is in the "darkness or lower level of consciousness," I must be aware of this so that I may give it no energy and hold strong in my commitment to God.

Without discernment, one is susceptible to negative energy, especially through your compassionate help. This is not to say that you must not use compassion and love in helping someone. However, you do not allow yourself to be tricked by their energy. This is where the distinction between judgment and discernment comes in. Judgment is the act of separating yourself from the other person and discernment is simply acknowledging their position and staying in love and compassion.

Listening to our messages, once we receive them is also crucial in determining how to proceed. There are four ways in which we receive our messages from Spirit: Knowing, Seeing, Feeling and Hearing. Everyone has a circuit in which Spirit talks to them through their intuition.

This circuit is much like that of a parent waking their child for school. Usually the child *knows* it is time to awaken. However, if they do not listen, then, that brings about the second message of their parent entering the room in a physical fashion standing over them so they may see them. If that still does not awaken them, there may come a resounding touch or *feeling* and, of course, lastly, a sharp *voice* that will, if all else fail, awaken the sleeping child.

God speaks to us in somewhat the same fashion through our intuition. My experience is that when I listen to God through my *knowing* and do not doubt or choose to ignore the message, it will suffice. However, many times I have fallen into doubt or literally choose not to listen because I did not like the message I was receiving. Then, I will experience the next message through my *visual* senses and this will continue until all circuits have been used to get the message across. This is much like we, as parents, will do with our own children. It is much more pleasant to get the message the first time.

Let me give you an example of using discernment. Let's say you decide to color your hair a completely different color from what is your natural coloring. The hairdresser asks what your original color is, not to judge whether your hair is indeed the color you say, but to discern exactly what colors are needed to mix for the intended result. If you say you are blonde and your roots clearly show brunette, it would be horrendous for you, your hair and your hairdresser if, in taking your word, he or she judges what you say instead of using discernment and doing what they know to do.

This brings up one of many circumstances that

I have had regarding discernment. People are on the path of spiritual awakening and even though they come to me as a client willing to heal the hurts, many times they are too frightened or ashamed to bring up their issues because they feel I may judge them as wrong. If I operated in my logical mind I, most likely, would hold a judgment regarding what they have done. However, Michael will give me the truth of their heart so that I know exactly what path to take which best serves in healing their issue. When your heart is engaged it is impossible to judge anything.

I started my career professionally working with a client, Pam, who also became a dear friend. At the time, it was a sticky situation even with discernment. In one particular session, the lines between friendship and that of client were somewhat unclear and I was accused of stifling her spiritual growth. Intuitively, Pam knew that she would be doing work in the field of spirituality using her intuition. She felt that the time had come.

Michael very clearly told me that she needed more time for growth and to build confidence in herself and that she was not yet ready to move forward in that direction. I relayed the message I had been given and although I knew it came from a place of discernment, Pam misinterpreted it as my judging her intuitive abilities.

I became the accused. Pam believed my intent was to hold her down and keep her from being an equal. I did, indeed, *know* she would be doing intuitive work, only in what vein I was not sure. Yet, had I encouraged her to take that step at that time in her life, it would have been devastating to her emotionally, mentally and physically.

I left the session swirling with anger and betrayal. After all, I was simply doing what I was guided to which was to help people develop their intuitive abilities while ensuring safety at the same time. I knew our friendship, at least for the time being, had come to an end.

It was difficult and uncomfortable to stay committed to my Higher Consciousness when it appeared that I was losing dear friends and a moment of doubt crept in. I questioned if perhaps I was truly judging or if what she said held any truth for I know anger is a reaction to judgment and I was indeed angry. What I realized the truth to be was not anger at my friend for the accusation. It was anger at Michael for putting me in a position in which I had to be the one to tell her to slow down.

I have had many exhausting conversations with Michael regarding my commitment to God and serving him in this capacity. I came to understand why this was a crucial lesson I needed to learn. Without discernment in this work and in life, it can be disastrous to oneself as well as those with whom you come in contact. Michael helped me to clearly understand the distinction between discernment and judgment as well as releasing attachments to other people's behaviors. The lessons here were priceless, yet, they cost me my friendship.

The blessing behind what appears to be disappointment, anguish and sadness is the miraculous gifts that follow. Eight months later Pam called me and we worked through all that had transpired between us. Our friendship became stronger for this experience. Pam has since worked diligently on herself through various healers – healing the hurts and filling her heart.

She has, indeed, found her calling through spiritual healing. Although the methods to which we approach our gifts of healing are different, she is ready to handle anything that comes her way. I now gladly refer clients to her and she to me.

12

Victims-There Are None

We are responsible *only* for ourselves – our words, deeds and actions. We have responsibilities, but we are responsible for our own person. When you make yourself responsible for anyone other than yourself, a mentality of fear says something outside of yourself has made this choice without your consent. We all possess the ability to be powerful beings. If you believe to any extent that someone or something outside of you can do anything that is out of your control, then, you have forfeited your power of connection to that belief and not to God.

This happens so often and in so many ways. Examples of this are when you give someone the right to ruin your day by cutting you off in traffic, struggling with an argument before leaving for work or school in the morning or in sensing someone else's negative energy and taking it on yourself.

Of course, this includes even the big things in our lives such as divorce, sexual assault, robbery and killing. These are just a few examples of things that occur which immediately cause us to lose our connection or "power" to God. The mere act of doing this starts the process of being the victim.

I am not saying that perpetrators of crimes should not be held accountable for their actions. However, to claim that you are powerless over these circumstances in your life, causes the action of becoming a victim. You always have a choice to use these experiences in a growing manner for a much fuller experience of life. To be a victim stops the process and the growth.

I learned at the age of seven that life was more complicated than I thought it to be. It started with the car rides with my grandfather. My dad's father died when Dad was fourteen from a heart attack. Grandma remarried and they moved here to Phoenix. Grandpa Ken was the only grandfather I ever knew. Lisa and I justified the things he did to us as being not so bad because he wasn't our "real" grandpa. Somehow calling him "step-grandpa" made it seem easier.

He would pick me up in his 1964 beige Cadillac while my grandmother waited for us at the house. "It" would only occur if my sister was not along for the ride. At the time I didn't know "it" was happening to her, too. He began fondling me whenever we were alone or if we were at his house and my grandma was in the back room ironing or napping.

The strangest part of it was that neither he nor I said a word. It was as if it wasn't really happening – dead silence. My thoughts would run rampant, "What is he doing? This is wrong! What do I do? I'm scared."

I said nothing to anyone about what was happening. He never threatened me or told me not to tell my parents or Grandma. It was just understood that I was to say nothing. I closed off a portion of my heart, becoming numb – somehow putting myself into a trance until it was over. Although he was physically molesting me, he never hurt me physically, which is to say, we never had intercourse.

This experience continued sporadically until the beginning of sixth grade. By this time my sister and I knew Grandpa was "playing," as he referred to it, with both of us. Whenever we were to spend the night at my grandparents, we would come up with reasons not to go over there. When we did, we would stay close to our grandma so we didn't have to be alone with him. This method seemed to work as the incidents became few and far between until they just faded away. That is until my parents went out of town.

My grandparents came to the house to watch

us and I had a friend stay the night. Grandpa tried to molest my friend. I was devastated. When she told me what happened I thought I died inside. My heart was so hurt. I thought this was a thing of the past. How dare he humiliate me in front of one of my friends? I was livid inside and horribly embarrassed. I had handled the issues I had with my grandpa. I was no longer his victim and now he had, once again, crossed the line.

In trying to perpetrate his sickness onto my friend, I felt hatred and disgust for him all over again. It was as though I had put it behind me and he brought it right back to the surface. I told my sister about what had happened and for the first time we went to our parents and told them what he had been doing to us over the years. It's funny how we value others more than ourselves and are willing to speak up when we see them being "victimized," than we are willing to when we experience it for ourselves.

My parents took care of the situation and although it wasn't until years later that we were given details as to how they resolved it, we were instructed by our parents never to go near him again. He was still around, but an adult was always present. My parents did not make him pay for his crime behind bars, yet he did have consequences. All that we appreciated in him, his intelligence and wit and all that had been held in high esteem were no longer respected nor sought after. He paid dearly for his actions in the solitude that lasted the rest of his life.

I knew it was up to me to carry myself as victim or victor. I chose to learn from the molestation, never again agreeing to other's silent secrets. It served me well, years later, when an unknown person was stalking me. Every morning before work I would see the same man at the same time following me. He would dart in and out of traffic just to get behind me or to the side of me in traffic. He made it very obvious that he wanted his presence known to me.

I was not sure of his intent exactly; only that he was very blatant in his attempts to intimidate me with fear. Instead of being afraid, I spoke with my dad who told me to get his license plate number. After doing so, he called a police officer that he knew and had it traced. By the following day, the man had been contacted, warned and never showed up around me again.

Many times we put ourselves into a victim role – expecting the worse and getting it. We need to regain our connection with God and know that we are never victims of circumstance. Every time I think I've mastered the concept of creating my own reality,

I'm given yet another opportunity to prove it. Once again, Michael gave me an experience that I would rather have learned differently – in a less painful way.

My dear friend, Holly, is a consultant in the candle business and invited me to join her at one of her bookings. We had conducted "candle/angel" parties before and it seemed to be a welcome addition to her business as well as a way for me to promote mine. It began with the usual pleasantries and introductions after which Holly gave her presentation.

Once Holly concluded her portion of the evening, many of the ladies present began asking questions about my work and the connection that I have with angels, spirits, etc. Things seemed to be going along as usual – telling a little about myself and how I got started as well as how their own intuitive abilities could be developed further. As I have said, doing this type of work requires my heart to be wide open so I may accurately and precisely align with Michael and any spirits present who are wishing to communicate.

Suddenly, I felt an enormous amount of negative energy emanating from one of the guests in particular and knew immediately that she was very confronted with my presence. Working with people and their skepticism is part of the process until they can discern for themselves the authenticity behind my work. I engaged in a conversation with this woman to what I thought was openness on her part toward my work. It seemed as though she was interested in what I was saying to the group of ladies. However, at the very same time, I was feeling a strong judgment from her toward me.

I asked whether she disagreed with what I was saying or had any questions that could clarify the open disdain she was feeling toward me. This is where it got a little hairy. It was my understanding that everyone at the party was open to me being there along with my work and my sharing it with them. This, I found out, was not exactly the case. She knew I was going to be there and wanted to observe. I am willing to have people observe my methods for I do not condemn or judge other's beliefs of faith and, naively, I believed the same would be reciprocated.

I told her that if it was her wish for me to refrain from any interaction with her, I was willing to honor those feelings. At the same time, I requested that she also honor my presence, as well as the other guests who wished to interact, by abstaining from communication with me both verbally and mentally. She agreed, got up and went into the kitchen. However, when you're open to universal energy, it doesn't matter if you're physically out of sight or not. The presence of that energy is all around. So, naturally, the conflict, which has been silently created, still hangs in the air.

When she came back into the room all seemed to be going well. Yet, I was continually brought back to her overwhelming energy. Finally, she explained her position and it was then that I found out she was devoutly religious. She explained to me that she did, indeed, believe from the accuracy of what she was hearing that I was undoubtedly communicating with angels and spirits. However, I was, "wrong for doing so."

I asked her why she stayed around after the candle presentation if she felt I was wrong or was she merely there to judge me? She said she was not judging me. She was interested in what I had to say. I explained that being interested when you have already condemned someone to being wrong is judgment.

Completely taken aback, yet, recognizing I was in somebody's home, I tried to be considerate of her beliefs while, at the same time, honoring my own. I had been doing workshops by this time, but always in my own home – in my own surroundings. This confrontation left me feeling vulnerable and exposed – as though I was being fed to the lions.

The force of the energy felt through this woman's condemnation and judgment, overwhelmed me to such an extent that I instantly went to a place of hurt, fear and vulnerability. I had been assured that I was welcomed and now felt like a cruel joke had been played on me and that Michael had perpetrated it.

I felt as a stripper might feel – doing a strip tease only to look down and find that I was not in a bar, but in a church. A stripper in a strip bar is completely appropriate. Stripping in a church – the complete opposite.

I closed off tightly. I felt like crying and running. Also, as I mentioned, I felt betrayed by Michael. I pleaded, "Why didn't you tell me this was going to occur?"

Holly and I were out of there in a hurry. She was frantically packing her candles as I was putting on a very strong face and saying my good-byes. Although I knew the others were interested in what I had to offer, I couldn't get to the car fast enough. I burst out into tears. I experienced every emotion possible–fear, vulnerability, hatred for this part of me that was multi-dimensional and anger directed at Michael.

I felt like a complete victim of some sick trick to expose me and open me to great ridicule. My childhood experiences were running rampant in my mind. Upon later reflection, I understood what Michael was showing me. I still had a part of my wounded mind that said to me, "You are wrong if you do not believe in the eyes of religion."

I know that not to be true now, since religion is

merely a much more restricted method of knowing God that is beneficial to many people. I simply do not fit into the category of needing a lot of external discipline. I have always been very self-disciplined. I felt victimized by this circumstance while going through it.

However, I know how much that wound needed to be healed before I further exposed myself to larger groups of people who may hold very different views than my own. I now can look back with gratitude that Michael chose that environment to reveal my wound and not a larger arena, however painful it was that day.

13
Spiritual Guides –
Who Are They?

I begin this chapter with a story of how I began to really understand not only Archangel Michael but other guides as well. I was deep into my spiritual quest, living a life of intuitive bliss with Jeff through the sharing of our heart connection. I had completed a course helping me gain a deeper understanding of how to develop intuition through a method called kinesiology and was beginning to see the results in my life.

Throughout the different courses, seminars and studies I had been evaluating, I also began evaluating my life, where it was going and where I wanted it to go. I knew I wanted to continue working. Yet, I wanted more time with my two boys.

One summer, I got a message from Michael to call Jacob's school about setting him up for the new school year. I spoke with the Administrative

Coordinator regarding his enrollment and just as we were about to hang up she told me she was moving out of state and thought I would be a great candidate for her job. I wasn't interested as I didn't want to work full time, but after some persuasion she convinced me of the benefits to working there and I agreed to meet with her.

I didn't know at the time that this was an instrumental building block in furthering my spiritual journey. I saw it as an opportunity to be with my children during the day and still make some money. "Coincidentally," the school also moved their location and instead of driving them eight miles through the heart of the town during rush hour traffic, I would be driving only a half a mile.

At the interview, I met the man I would be working for directly, Edgar Ball. I knew immediately Edgar was not only one of the main reasons I was drawn to taking the job. I knew he was also the icing on the cake and, without a doubt, was going to be a dear friend who would teach me many things I probably would not learn elsewhere. Our friendship grew from that point forward.

Edgar and I had instant rapport as administrator and assistant, yet, our relationship became more of a spiritual mentor/protege collaboration. Edgar is highly intelligent, as well as intuitive, and through him I was allowed to see how the mind and spirit work together. One afternoon, at lunch, we were discussing work when, suddenly, the conversation turned to spirituality and spirit guides. I sensed two guides with us, one an Indian chief and the other a woman and told Edgar about their presence. Edgar wasn't the least bit surprised and said he had known for many years that Yellow Eagle and Kuan Yin are with him. I was elated.

Here was a man whose opinion I very much respected, confirming I wasn't "out there." We spoke of our guides–who they are, where they come from and what purpose they serve in our lives. This was only the beginning of many talks that helped each of us grow further in our spirituality and I knew I needed to introduce Edgar to the women in my "group" that had been meeting every other week for years.

In 1992, Mom, Lisa and I went to California to attend a "woman's weekend" workshop with 200 other woman from all over the country. In this weekend, we learned how to honor and cherish who we are personally as women, how we interact with other women and our perceived relationships with men. I took this course as one of my "last ditch" efforts to help save my first marriage. Ultimately, my marriage faltered. However, the course did, indeed, help me in acknowledging that self-respect and honor of myself needs to come first always.

The three of us realized we needed to continue supporting one another, as well as other women, in the endeavors of our lives. We formed a group, together with the friend that had introduced us to this work, and have been meeting ever since. Over the years some of the faces have moved on and we've added new ones, but the bonds that we've built with these women are stronger than ever.

By the time I met Edgar, our growth had become a bit stagnant. I knew that inviting him into our group, with his wealth of knowledge, would alter and expand the dynamics of our spiritual group as well as continue to encompass the support of our various relationships. The group welcomed him with open arms and what was once referred to as our "women's group" became "group."

I do not facilitate this group. I have worked with everyone privately in sessions or through the workshops I lead. However, in our group this is set aside and we share our intuitive abilities with one another as a whole. It is a safe place for us all to share our fears and victories. Undeniably, the foundation we have built with one another has given us the courage and strength to get through many trials and tribulations while sharing the joys of everyday life.

I first allowed Michael's communication to be known in this group and their confidence, patience and support enabled me to hone my abilities, just as each of them were building communication with their own guides. The respect we have for one another is mutual and highly regarded.

Learning the language of our guides is a lot like learning Spanish, when all you know is English. It starts out slow and unclear, "foreign," in every sense of the word, until you understand the basics of the language and start building from there. At first, you're hearing Spanish; translating it in your head to English and then speaking it back in Spanish. Much patience and fine-tuning are needed but, then, before you know it, you're not only speaking Spanish, you're bilingual.

Since every individual has their own guide and we're not all guided by the same one, I would like to explain how guides come to us and how they each have a common theme unto themselves. I will list the guides individually along with the participants in the group that they guide, along with an example of how they have received and benefited from their messages. My hope is for you to perhaps recognize any similarities and see the distinctions in your own lives.

Archangel Michael: Overcoming Adversity

People guided by Michael can attest to the adversity that comes in great proportions. Overcoming these adversities is our greatest challenge. We tend to become very closed off even appearing cold hearted at times when we choose not to take his challenge and push through it. We may go through a long period of time simply being stuck, somewhat like that of a defiant child, knowing what needs to be done and refusing to do it.

I feel certain that, at these times, Michael must be laughing at us, waiting patiently for us to align with his energy so we can once again push through whatever we've allowed to hold us back. The moment we do make a decision to align and be open for the truth, we move forward very rapidly. Michael carries a high intensity of energy and if you allow it to come through, you will find he's masterful at manifesting what you desire, once you listen. Here are examples of those in our group guided by Michael.

I met Holly at the christening of my goddaughter, Bailey. Instantly, we became fast friends, as though we had known one another our entire lives. She joined our group around the end of 1999 and the joy she has brought can only be described as infectious. Watching Holly in action is absolutely amazing. She knows and embraces the powerful energy Michael provides her and is determined not to let adversity stop her from manifesting her heart's desire.

When she is confronted with something contrary to her well being and is unwilling to face it, she usually retracts within herself. It sometimes appears as though the presence of joy is still surrounding her, but if you take a closer look, the sparkle in her eye is not so bright and the music in her voice not as sweet. Fortunately, she is very in tune with Michael's presence and can usually find her center quickly.

Holly brings to the group the ability to see and obtain our own desires of the heart, regardless how steep the path may appear. She will not stand for anyone even entertaining the thought that their hearts desire's are impossible. Holly's truth that God is "All There Is" and the way in which she proclaims that truth, inspires many through the pure joy of being in her presence.

Besides Holly and myself, Michael also guides Cindy Bates. Cindy is relatively new to our group and the change in her since making the decision to align with Michael's energy is incredible. Cindy's adversity comes through in challenges with her weight. Consciously, and with an undaunted determination to heal the wounds that caused her protective weight gain, Cindy is determined to let nothing get in the way of being her authentic self once again. The willingness to look adversity in the face, through healing past issues, was all she needed for the weight to melt away like butter. Cindy is masterful in producing the results she desires and her courage has been inspiring.

Archangel Gabrielle: Seeing Opposing Views

Gabrielle has a unique way of giving *all* views. His primary field of expertise is aligning with those that have a difficult time knowing who they are in relationships. Most people guided by Gabrielle are here to show both sides of any situation, to be a mediator. An example could be that of a news reporter whose job it is to see all sides of the story and remain neutral. This is the challenge for those guided by Gabrielle because, when they do take sides, they can appear very critical or judgmental. When in alignment, however, they are very loving, wonderful listeners who often dispense sound advice.

Gabrielle is also a trickster. Many times he will trick people into action when they have left neutral ground and chosen sides. Here are the people in our group guided by Gabrielle and some of the lessons we have learned through them.

My mom, Sandy, is not only a wonderful asset for her listening abilities, but also for her ability to show us different ways to see things, as she did in her quest to quit smoking. Mom and I were in a session when my Grandma Bette, who passed away in 1974, came to me relaying the message that Mom was in danger of getting emphysema. The reaction to her mother's message was startling to me until I learned why. At a recent doctor's appointment, her doctor had given her the very same message. Prior to this, Gabrielle had let her know it was time to stop smoking. Now it was twice confirmed. With Gabrielle's help, I guided her through the process of quitting.

After 38 years of smoking and various attempts throughout those years to quit, success could be measured in anywhere from a couple weeks to about four months before she would continue the habit once again. Needless-to-say, Mom preferred the quickest, easiest and less challenging method available. The instructions given to us by Gabrielle were very specific, not that easy and extremely challenging.

Two weeks from the day of the session, on a Saturday, Mom was instructed to buy a carton of strong, unfiltered cigarettes and smoke one after another until the carton was gone. Immediately, she chose the way of logic and a multitude of reasons why she didn't really need to stop smoking presented themselves. Incredulous at what was being asked of her, she wondered if it was really worth it and whether there was *anyone* on this planet actually capable of physically fulfilling what Gabrielle was instructing her to do! Putting logic aside, she asked Gabrielle if this method was indeed her path and, after affirming its accuracy, followed through with his instructions, consequences and all.

True to form of anyone guided by Gabrielle and choosing not to stay neutral, Mom went in and out of panic. Throughout the week her mind would come up with horrific scenarios about what she could expect. During this time, she received a phone call from her aunt and uncle saying they would be in town for the weekend and that they would like to stay with her and Dad. Mom was elated.

The visit was a true gift from God since this particular aunt has always been a great spiritual inspiration and mentor to her–someone who, as it happens, is also guided by Gabrielle. The two of them made plans to be together on the day mom was to begin the process of quitting her smoking. Knowing she wouldn't have to go through this experience alone was enough for Mom to change her perception and actually see the possibility of success.

On that fateful Saturday, I received a phone call. Mom was riddled with angst. Plans had fallen through and it was no longer just she and her aunt. It appeared that every time the path was cleared, circumstances placed yet another seemingly unavoidable obstacle in front of her that kept throwing her back into logic. The task at hand looked too huge and painful to undergo. We discussed where her anxieties came from and how, at times, Gabrielle has a warped sense of humor when showing the opposing view, especially, when his messages are received with an unwillingness to stay neutral.

I encouraged her to focus on her desire to give up cigarettes and reassured her of God and Gabrielle's presence throughout the process. Amazingly enough the message changed and Gabrielle, the trickster, had now determined she only had to smoke three packs of cigarettes in quick succession. This did little to assuage her mind. Three packs or a carton, what was the difference? The two both screamed, "Impossible!"

Mom did, however, accept her message, found neutral ground and started smoking. Three cigarettes later, she was in her backyard puking her guts out and wondering how she was going to lift another cigarette to her lips, let alone smoke it! The message came through, loud and clear, that her task was complete.

The enormity of Gabrielle's message and Mom's perception of it sent her into such calamity that she wasn't able to see the simplicity of what it could be. The trickster had come to call again. Mom's test was whether she could stay neutral to the message she had been given or if she was going to choose sides and live in the chaos of her own mind.

When Mom finally chose to accept the message without any judgments, she was let off the hook. She also learned that she was strong enough in her connection to physically go through this alone without anybody holding her hand and telling her that all would be okay. The trust she placed in herself and Gabrielle resulted in her heart's desire to be a non-smoker. I am pleased to announce that she has been smoke-free for over three years and a true inspiration to us all!

LuVerna Manuel has been with our group since day one and her dedication to the unity of the group is undisputed. The characteristics of Gabrielle can be seen in both LuVerna and my mom. However, LuVerna has such a thirst for learning that at times it is difficult for her to stay neutral because of her extensive knowledge.

LuVerna's desire is to purchase a home here in Arizona, a desire that has been ongoing and one she intends to fulfill. She first began by acknowledging the desire, then, started envisioning the home itself.

At one point, she was guided to the area, price range, realtor and lender. She actively pursued her messages.

Then, as usually happens when pursuing our dream, issues started arising. She and her husband disagreed on what they desired in a house and the homes did not have what they wanted. There are myriads of things we come up with as individuals or as couples when making such a commitment. Thus, began her long battle with logical mind games, both active and in ready-play.

LuVerna and her husband have traveled and lived all over the world, even owning LuVerna's dream house, although in another state. She received the message that she could, yet again, have her heart's desire here. Only, her logic questioned that possibility and she stepped off her neutral ground and into the chaos of choosing sides. Once there, it is very difficult to get out of it unless you willingly become neutral and allow spirit to draw you out.

LuVerna's challenge is in remembering to honor herself in her relationships with people—asking for what she wants and knowing that she is worthy of receiving it. This is a crucial step and one she is consciously taking. She has become neutral once again and allows all views to be seen while staying neutral to the outcome. LuVerna has broadened her approach at buying her new home and awaits Gabrielle's next message. Having seen and experienced the manifestations of LuVerna's heart, I know it will truly be magnificent.

Last, but not least, is Mary Ann Hillman. Mary Ann dreamed of opening a Montessori School. She knew the name and had a good feeling for the energy that would surround it. Though it took years to manifest, she held strongly to her vision. Gabrielle guided her to the location and she found the building of her dream or, at least, the potential of her dream. *The Center for Creative Education* was born.

In purchasing the building, Mary Ann experienced some struggle staying neutral to the messages she received. Yet, all in all, she kept coming back to her inner truth and succeeded. The difficulties confronting her after acquiring the building, however, were enough to send anyone packing. Fortunately, whenever she thought there was no way to pull it off, she drew on her experience, communication and success with Gabrielle during the beginning stages of the project.

Mary Ann's success in listening and following through with her messages, helped her to appreciate the benefits of all the people and circumstances around her in making this building not only usable, but beautiful, too. Mary Ann is an inspiring testament to the truly incredible work of someone allowing Gabrielle to guide her.

Jesus: Acceptance & Love

The relationship between Jesus and the people who are guided by him is different than that of the traditional religious point of view. We are all being guided by Jesus' loving example of who we are aspiring to be while walking this human path. However, when Jesus is your guide, there is a different experience than that of who he is for us in the biblical sense.

If Jesus is your guide, you can bet you have a tendency to want to control everything in your life. When not listening to his divine guidance, you are busy believing that you are controlling your world. You cease to create your reality and become dogmatic about life–falling into mental rules and regulations.

Once you move to a space of self-acceptance and love, watch out! It is like listening to a beautiful orchestra with the right instrument playing at the right time making an amazing concerto. People guided by Jesus become fabulous healers, role models and examples of what others aspire to become.

Darvina Nogales was a novice when she joined our group. She was lost in the concepts and jargon we used such as universal energy, human consciousness or the various ways of receiving messages and so remained quiet. She took it all in, while at the same time, working diligently at understanding and embracing her own self-awareness. She saw the rules she had established in her life which kept her from fully living. Once she moved into a space of love and acceptance of herself, showed us all what it looks like when you heal the inner wounds and begin to create what you want out of life.

Darvina wanted another child to share in her life and that of her 10-year-old son. She wanted to raise them in a small town. Her heart said, "go for it." Her standards or inner rules said that you couldn't do that without a man. Within a year, every thing began falling into place simultaneously. She became pregnant. Another member of our group was moving out of state and had a house in a little town north of Phoenix that they wanted to rent. Without knowing where she was going to work, Darvina rented their house and moved.

Once there, she realized her small pickup truck wasn't ideal for herself and her children and that she would have to create a family car. Not knowing how she was going to create this with a new job and limited budget she stated her desires and gave it up to God. Amazingly, and, yet, not surprisingly, she was given a 1998 four-door car with payments that fit her budget.

Darvina gave up control of how it was *supposed* to happen and, though unconventional as it appeared, she and God co-created in manifesting the desires of her heart. Of course, this did not come without some bumps in the road and questioning of herself from time to time. However, her commitment was authentic and she produced the intended results.

Jeffrey Steed has now been with our group a few years. Jeffrey is an educator whose profession is typically known for examining issues and situations through the use of intellect and analysis. Jeffrey has proven this approach to be both an asset and a hindrance in regard to his intuitive abilities. Becoming acquainted with Jesus and his messages was a difficult process for him in the beginning. He fought with many logical mind issues, trying to control his thoughts and, in the process, lost his ability to live from his heart.

Once Jeffrey dealt with the rules and regulations of all he had been taught and had stored in his mind, he found, with Jesus' guidance, that he could go beyond his logic and balance it with his heart to accept and love himself. Jeffrey is extremely expressive and I believe his rules of how he thought he should conduct himself suppressed the expression of fun and excitement that wanted to come spilling from his heart.

If there was anyone who was dogmatic about how it was "supposed to be," it was Jeffrey. From the moment he joined our group until now, Jeffrey's assiduousness to break through his self-imposed beliefs has been nothing short of astounding. In lessening the hold on his life that he felt driven to control, he found himself trying new things such as auditioning and landing a role in a local theater production. He is now a part of that theater company. The acceptance Jeffrey has gained for himself has proven to be one of inspiration for us all. What a dramatic shift!

George Hillman is an incredible artist as well as a hands-on healer. Allowing himself to be seen, known and acknowledged for these gifts has been very challenging. George is a retired Air Traffic Controller/Enroute Flight Advisory Specialist. When Michael told me he was guided by Jesus, I found myself tickled by the term "controller" since that is the characteristic which is hardest for people guided by Jesus to overcome, and most assuredly for George.

George also had imposed great rules and regulations on himself, especially in the area of his hands-on healing and art work. As difficult and challenging as it has been for him, he has begun to show himself as the gifted healer God intended him to be while working with friends and family in developing his gift.

Mother Mary: Nurturing

Mother Mary, as she is depicted in the bible, is true to who she is as a guide, also. She is there to nurture, support and motivate those in which she guides with whatever means possible to accomplish that goal. As she guided Jesus into his calling from God to fulfill his duties on Earth, she also does so for those to whom she is a personal guide. The most important part to understand, however, is that without self-nurturing there is nothing to give. Those guided by Mother Mary will become insecure and self-doubting – *second-guessing every move* they make if they do not first nurture themselves.

We have several women in our group (Lisa, Page, Sandy and Patti) who are guided by Mother Mary. My sister, Lisa, is a woman you want on your side. She allows people in her life to move to great heights while nurturing them along the way. This, however, does not always look like the conventional view of nurturing. When Lisa gets a message, beware! You will know it. Many times her nudging of us to become all that we can be, feels confronting and abrasive – anything but nurturing. You can count on her to make sure you do not stay stagnant for long. Lisa simply says it like it is and does exactly what is needed without second-guessing herself.

Many times Lisa is not even aware that she is receiving a message from Mother Mary. However, when she is in a place where her own self-nurturing has been put on the back burner, she will begin self-destructive behavior. In these instances, she second-guesses herself without knowing or acknowledging that she is doing it. She must remain conscious of what will nurture her in any given situation to keep herself in alignment.

Page McGee is a school teacher with a heart of gold, whose students thrive under her loving attention. Page is a person who tends to put the needs of others before herself. In second-guessing her messages from Mother Mary, we, as a group, have watched her accommodate people at the expense of her self-esteem. Her desire for approval and avoidance of confrontation was put to the test when administrators, parents and teachers became pitted against one another over certain school issues.

Page found herself in a quandary of wanting to please everyone. Determination to put her needs first and follow her intuitive messages, is what moved her through self-deprecation to a resolution of what needed to be done for the children. In consciously being aware of her needs and her tendency to second-guess herself, Page has become a woman of great strength

– achieving her desires and uplifting many of her students along the way. Nurturing yourself will always result in the nurturing of those around you.

As was revealed in our first session, Sandy Jenkins' intuitive abilities come to her visually. She saw beautiful colors of light coming from the top of my head and connecting through our hearts. Sandy's visions often show the outcome of her messages. Unfortunately, many times she would second-guess the vision, doubt the message and create self-destructive behavior and feelings of insecurity.

Sandy had the vision of being in a committed, long-term relationship with a person she barely knew. She pursued the relationship even though the other person did not feel the same way at the time. Sandy stayed focused and, in time, the union became a reality. Sometime during their courtship, she started second-guessing herself, trusting, instead, the opinions of others and denying her own intuition as to whether this was, indeed, "forever."

As a result, the relationship began to falter. This is typical of people guided by Mother Mary. They tend to value other's messages more than their own. Finally, Sandy stopped the chatter in her mind, refocused her vision and intent. She reclaimed her connection with Mother Mary, her relationship and the vision that she had from the beginning, allowing the relationship to flourish.

I personally received the benefits of Patti Cranson's ability to nurture and support other people when purchasing my home. Patti assisted me as my realtor and did not let my lack of finances get in the way. Her message was clear, "get Lynn into a house and do not let anything stop you." Many times I would go to my logical mind, writing down addresses I thought would fit my desire for size, quality and location, within the price range for which we were pre-qualified. Patti was doing everything possible to accommodate and nurture me through this process despite my frustration in accomplishing my goal.

When she finally got tired of following *my* messages, she stopped second-guessing her own and chose to nurture herself by closing the deal. Patti was guided to pull up a different list of houses in an area that appeared to be completely out of the realm of our qualifications. She found the most beautiful home, far exceeding my own expectations and, at the same time, meeting my "unheard of" move-in date. Approximately two weeks after first setting eyes on my home, escrow was closed and I was setting up house–in the world of real estate, a miracle, indeed!

Chamuel: Adoration & Growth

Chamuel is about adoration of God through self,

bringing growth on all levels. Once self-adoration is mastered, those guided by Chamuel will have a renowned ability to see beauty in any situation and stimulate growth spiritually, physically and intellectually.

Carla Trujillo is our only member guided by Chamuel and represents beauty and growth in their truest forms. Her messages, although discreet, are played out in the most beautiful way. Carla has a wonderful husband, two incredible children and always wanted another child to complete her idea of how a family would feel.

When I first met Carla a few years ago, she had become pregnant. Unfortunately or fortunately, when seen in the overall context of her life, she lost the baby. Carla became very lost and began questioning this time in her life, losing adoration for herself and how God was working in and through her.

Once Carla stopped manipulating her perception of what losing the baby meant, she was able to forgive herself, move past the experience and grow from it. Through embracing her own self-adoration and God, Carla gave birth recently to a healthy, beautiful daughter, Victoria Anna.

Kuan Yin: Compassion

Kuan Yin has many of the same characteristics of Mother Mary with one exception. You must be in a space of compassion when aligning to her. If you are not in alignment, you will appear extremely critical to others and your self-doubting games will begin.

Edgar Ball has several examples of how Kuan Yin works through him. But, one incident, in particular, jumps out at me. Edgar was renting a house in Clarkdale, Arizona. The person from whom he was renting was returning, giving him very little time to find a new place. As usual, Edgar put off looking for other lodgings until the eleventh hour. He regularly asks and receives clear messages from Kuan Yin and asked her the price range, location, etc. of where to go. Then, he set out combing the newspaper. Most people would call this waiting until the last minute. However, as I said, Edgar knows Kuan Yin intimately and has complete trust in her guidance.

Edgar found something in Jerome that seemed to meet his needs and set up an appointment to meet the realtor at a gas station near the bottom of the hill leading to Jerome. On the day of the appointment, he pulled up next to a yellow Cadillac with a woman in it. Edgar said something to the effect that he was ready to see the place.

After she answered his question, indicating she understood him, he followed her up the hill in his own car. The woman went straight to the area the newspaper had listed, pulled into the garage and got out. Edgar pulled in behind her and asked to see the apartment. The woman looked at him as if he was addle-minded. She didn't have any idea what he was talking about or why he had followed her.

After apologizing profusely and feeling very stupid, Edgar drove back to his office in Clarkdale and called the realtor. She was fuming. She had waited for him at the gas station only to be blown-off, or so she thought, and basically wasn't willing to help him any further. This is at the point where being compassionate in your alignment with Kuan Yin comes in. Even though he was still anxious about where he was going to live, Edgar found the humor in the situation and let all other mind chatter go.

Later that day, a woman for whom he was doing some graphics work, came in to the office. At some point during their conversation, his living situation came up. The woman happened to know someone whose mother was ailing and needed to rent her house out right away so she could move in and take care of her. Edgar called the woman and saw the house. Although the woman hadn't expected to move so soon, she said she would figure something out and agreed to rent the house to him. Edgar moved into a fully furnished house the very next day.

Had Edgar chosen to become critical, second-guessing himself over the incident in Jerome, he would have failed to find the house that was destined to be his and prolong the move that needed to take place immediately. Compassion and blind trust are a must when one is guided by Kuan Yin.

Angels, Spirit Guides or Ascended Masters

My understanding is that God gave us these guides to help us in our spiritual walk as he also gave us our parents for our human walk. I want to be clear that when I refer to the angels who assist me in my spiritual journey, I am fully aware that God is all I worship. However, I do respect and honor our guides and there place in my life.

All of us are guided by either an angel or an ascended master. God gives our personal guide to us for a specific reason. We all have a mission to accomplish while we are here on Earth. The guide who we have been given is assigned, for lack of a better term, to us for that mission or set of life lessons to which we agreed with God before our arrival on the Earth plane. Putting it into very simple terms, if our main mission in this life is to overcome strong adversities, you would be given Archangel Michael as your guide. He has many guides under him that are assisting you, also, though you may not know each of them on a one-on-one basis.

It is much like going to a specific college based upon what you desire to do for your profession. For example, if you wanted to be a dentist, you would choose a specific school that would benefit your career choice. God has made sure that who we are being guided by is directly related to each person's life purpose or mission. I have been given some specific characteristics of the guides with whom I have worked. These characteristics have been compiled from the work I have done with my clients over the years.

There are times I am very confronted by the fact that God gave me Michael. Each guide has predominant characteristics that are associated solely with each. Michael represents truth, honesty, integrity, the love for challenges and the overcoming of adversity. I know that the characteristics of our guides are the same characteristics we face within ourselves on this planet. It takes a lot of trust for me to rise to the occasion in serving Michael.

One of my first challenges was the blessing called Jeff. My husband was getting a little nervous about this new revelation that I had discovered called Archangel Michael. To him it was like I had just fallen off the spaceship and was telling him I was communicating with aliens regularly.

The truth is that aliens probably would have

been more accepted by him since he leans more toward science fiction reality. Angels were more than a little confronting. At first this was not a big deal because we were still sharing our hearts. However, that was going to change soon.

Jeff never became hurtful or violent, like my first husband. However, when I placed a judgment on myself as being different, I unfortunately directed it at him. I told him that if we didn't hold similar beliefs, especially with respect to God and spirituality, then, we couldn't make this marriage work. I became very judgmental and accused him of being unemotional, non-spiritual and of many other things. Our connection started to deteriorate and, without my husband to share my experiences as we had before, I was feeling scared and unsure of myself.

God gave us free will to choose and I had definitely made a choice to not look strange or different to anyone anymore. Except that now, I was 31 years old, on my second marriage and realized I couldn't deny my connection to God any longer. Looking back, I was so scared of this part of me. When I knew it was time to expand my communication with Michael to the outside world that included my family, friends and future clients, I became deathly afraid, just as that little girl had, years before, during her tea parties.

My experience of God, in terms of religion, was limited. My mother converted to Catholicism for my father's sake and they were married in a Catholic church. We went to church on most Sundays. My mother went to the church for the main mass and Lisa and I went to catechism. My father only attended church with us on Easter, Christmas and various other holidays. I received my First Communion even though I had no idea who God was.

My sister seemed to have a real grasp of "God." Lisa looked forward to going to church, attending classes and receiving her First Communion and Confirmation. My mother wanted Lisa to attend and conform to the foundation Catholicism offered. I perceived that Mom thought it was less important that I establish the same foundation. The part of me that felt unwanted at birth and not "good enough" resurfaced again.

Several years later I asked my mom why she didn't encourage my going to church as she had with Lisa. Her response was that she honestly did not know. She could actually see where the discipline of the church benefited Lisa. Yet, she didn't *feel* that it was necessary for me to pursue the same. It was later revealed to me, through Michael, that God and he work through my "knowing" and that the more I knew intellectually, the more I would second guess the "knowing" of my heart. That has been proven true time and time again.

Jeff was my first challenge to following the truth within me. Unfortunately, my logic prevailed and I thought the only path at that time was to separate from him so I could pursue my heart's dream of remembering God within me.

We sold our house, he moved in with friends and the boys and I moved in with my parents. Thank God that Adam and Jacob were sure of my connection with God and Michael, by this time, or things would have been even worse. Many times before, they had received proof that my connection with Archangel Michael and God was authentic. However, one particular incident before our separation clenched it for them.

Jeff had already gone to work and the boys and I woke up one morning to find our dog Sammy paralyzed on the floor of her sleeping room with her eyes puffed out. Her legs were stiff as boards and she was in great pain. She would whimper to the touch. We had no idea what was wrong with her. We thought perhaps a spider had bitten her.

I asked Michael, "What do I do?" He peacefully walked me through a step-by-step procedure. He directed me where to place my hands in order to draw the energy out of her legs and, then, to place my hands over her eyes. The process took approximately 10 to 15 minutes. Though it seemed like a lifetime. When Michael said to stop, she quickly jumped up and walked away as if nothing had happened.

Sammy never had a problem again. Jacob, Adam and I were simply astounded at the miracle we had just experienced. What made Sammy ill? I don't know. What I do know is that it was a test for me to follow through with my faith in Michael and God. This was just one of many instances we had experienced up to this point. My sons knew, I knew, so there was nothing to debate.

My husband, when told of this experience, was still not buying the whole angel story. Jeff and I still had contact during our separation. Neither of us was willing to start divorce proceedings. We still didn't agree on our paths. We were butting heads and every time I asked Michael whether or not I was to divorce Jeff, the answer was always "no."

Jacob and Adam learned how committed Jeff was to them in those months by their regular visitations with him. He didn't have to do that, quite frankly, because he was not legally responsible for them. The boys learned through this experience that their step-dad loved them beyond obligation.

It was five months into our separation before I could see the truth about how my judging myself and being right about my path was causing Jeff to question our marriage. He simply said to me one night, "I didn't marry Michael, I married you." I learned a huge lesson in not judging someone else's path to God when it doesn't match your own and Jeff learned how to forgive and open his heart to love once again.

I now know whatever Jeff's experience is of God, it is *his*, not mine, just as mine is not his. As fulfilling as it was for me to re-embrace this lost part of myself, he didn't understand. Jeff doesn't experience Angels or Spirits. The truth is that many people don't and may never let themselves.

Jeff is extremely artistic and drawn to the art of fabricating and using his intuition when it comes to machinery. I am not drawn to his intuitive path. We all have an intuitive side to our brain, but we may not use it in the same way. From that day forward, I could see his side of things. My mistake, if there even is such a thing, was judging my own path of spirituality as wrong because it didn't match his. He, in turn, became extremely defensive about his own experience and directed his judgment toward me.

The learning experience we all gained from these five months of separation was tremendous. One thing he knew was that he loved me and I knew I loved him. We agreed to disagree about our path of intuitive awakening. We also agreed that we both wanted to attempt to make this marriage work.

14
Spirit, Mind, Body Connection

Michael has guided me to four attributes of a person that helps us to achieve the Spirit, Mind, Body Connection. The first begins with a purely *loving, peaceful state* in which you feel comfort, divine love and safety. I find this state by communicating with Michael. Though, many people find it in a place or a circumstance that will assist them in getting there, such as a garden or possibly a safe relationship.

Once this loving state of existence is established, the second attribute that is evident is *clarity of messages*. Undeniably, clear messages are received as to what you need to do, accomplish or simply know for your forward movement. I first receive messages through my *knowing*. Then, a *visual* picture will be presented if I have any doubt in my *knowing*. Others receive their messages differently.

The third attribute is *no fear*. This is where most

people falter. The no-fear mode consists of letting go of any and all attachments to the message given. When you do not necessarily want or like the message you have been given, you will get stuck in this mode. This can last for a minute, day or even years.

I am well aware of this state since, throughout the years, I have been digging my feet in, so to speak, when I do not like the message or method to which I know I must go in order to further my growth. I knew, many years ago, when my husband Jeff and I separated, that I couldn't deny Michael's existence in our marriage for long. However, the fear of being divorced again and letting go of him did not sit well with me.

I stopped my growth in this area of my life deciding to deal with it later, hoping and waiting for either him to change or that, somehow, it would not matter. Neither occurred. We must remember that when we receive a divine message, the message does not change, no matter how much we want it to or try to stop it. It is a message from God not of our mind.

The fourth and final attribute is *living passionately* the message or vision you have received. This passion must come from a conviction that is unwavering. Along with the no-fear attribute, not living passionately is also where we get stuck. People will, at this point, begin questioning their message. This may be the hardest attribute to master as you must be so passionately drawn to your message that no one can pull you from believing it to be true.

This is where I have wavered many times. I did not have many people in my life, my husband included, that experienced angels as I had. I began limiting my experiences with Michael and the other angels so that it would be less confronting to my husband and others. From almost the beginning of my marriage to Jeff, I received a message that it was time to embrace my gift from God called intuition which, for me, *is* Archangel Michael.

People I both know and don't know have asked me many times, "Why can't you just refer to Michael as 'Spirit or intuition'?" This was asked of me in order not to look weird to others and I tried it as they suggested. The price, however, was my authenticity with myself – appeasing other's discomfort at the risk of my own integrity.

In order to shift to Spirit, Mind, Body, you must listen to your heart's desire instead of your mind's belief system. Your heart will give you an authentic desire to move you through a situation of judgment that perhaps the mind has stored as your belief, unwilling to be challenged. It becomes imperative that you *do*, in fact, challenge your mind's belief system.

Almost always, it is either someone else's truth laid upon you or an old wound stubbornly trying to hold on to the prison of the mind. This does not allow true freedom. All Mind, Body, Spirit connections will, at some point in your life, need to be transformed into Spirit, Mind, Body. This is the only authentic connection that will not give you pain and suffering. Pure wisdom is the way of Spirit, Mind, Body connection.

The heart uses the mind that, in turn, uses the body to manifest the heart's desire. This process begins with the concept that the heart is the place in which our true connection with God begins. The mind is the tool God has given us to discern the desires our heart is requesting to manifest. The logical mind, in its truest form without judgment or "positive side," will discern the best path to take in fully manifesting our heart's desire and without effort or strain.

The logical mind that has judgment is the so-called "negative side" of us or darkness. When we choose the path of darkness, we are establishing a right or wrong orientation to events in our life. Getting stuck here will create emotional wounds and pain from which we learn to clearly discern the path we want to take. Some individuals simply choose the path of least resistance by communicating with their heart, God, Angelic Realm, etc.

With great trust, they can move forward and manifest their heart's desire very quickly and easily. God has no attachment to which path we take. He gave us free will, which occurs in the logical mind, enabling us to learn through either the light or the dark.

Our logical mind, when it comes into contact with something it determines to be opposing to our belief system, must do only what it knows to do– choose judgment or discernment. If an emotional wound shows up that the logical mind can link to, it will surface so it can be understood and healed. It must, then, return to the past experiences so that the emotion can be cleared, allowing the heart to fulfill and manifest its desires.

If the opposition is denied by the mind and determined to be wrong, the mind will judge itself appearing as though it is judging others. The only reason we would believe the logical mind and make judgements is because of a disconnection from the heart or from God. The heart never feels pain or judges something as right or wrong. The mind is what is telling you to feel the emotion of pain or pleasure. If there is no past experience or teaching with which to relate, the mind will choose the path of discernment, manifesting the heart's desire as it was designed to do.

At the core of our existence, we are all diamonds. When our soul finds mud that has been slung on top of our bright and beautiful diamond, the natural reaction is to cleanse it. This is done in many ways. The most common way is to create a safe environment in which to speak your truth where judgment is not present. Unfortunately, many of us do not feel that there is a place in which this can be safely accomplished.

Therefore, we may engage in self-destructive behavior such as drinking, smoking, over-eating and many other forms of *mud-slinging*, choosing to live in the mind or *beneath the mud*, believing this will stop the pain our soul is attempting to purge and heal. What inevitably occurs is the strong desire to remove the inauthentic parts of us that are keeping our diamond from shining brightly. Fortunately and unfortunately this awakening sometimes only occurs after great pain and suffering. However, this no longer needs to be the only option.

I have a client who was living in Mind, Body, Spirit. She, through the course of our working together, transformed herself to Spirit, Mind, Body. At a time when I needed financial assistance to further my business, I was given the message that she was the one to assist me. This was confronting to me.

However, when I approached her with my need, she did not hesitate.

In the past, she would have questioned and worried about giving anyone a large sum of money since her experiences in this area had not benefited her. Her mind still felt the hurt of these experiences. To both of our amazement, there was no doubt that she was the one to assist me since she had clearly received the same message to do so. I have asked her to share a bit of her journey and how she now experiences life.

I feel very blessed to have the opportunity to share my transformation from Mind, Body, Spirit to Spirit, Mind, Body. This was very difficult as I was a person who was very analytical and analyzed every aspect of my life. I was living my life from my shoulders up, or more truthfully, between my ears. My mind controlled my life. It told me how to feel, when to hurt and what to do. My life was full of fear, shame, self-doubt, guilt, judgment and self-denial. It convinced me of things that weren't true and that I was a victim to everything that happened in my life. The idea that I was undeserving and should withhold my love from myself was self-taught with the help of my mind.

I was constantly punishing myself for past mistakes. I was my own worst enemy. I wanted to be perfect because, for my entire life, I was taught that only the people that are perfect are rewarded and will go to heaven. My belief system was well imprinted on me. I internalized all I was taught and didn't challenge it until recently.

I was raised a Methodist and never thought to explore other denominations. I changed churches from time-to-time, but never strayed from the faith. I would convince myself that a particular church was working for me even though I couldn't tell one thing that I liked about it. It wasn't bringing me fulfillment and I wasn't taking away any messages that applied to my life.

After months of forced participation and not finding enjoyment, I found Lynn. She didn't disparage the church or its beliefs. She helped me open up to the possibilities of expanding on what I'd already been taught and discerning which beliefs were the truth for me and which were not. Lynn's messages hit home and helped me to enhance my spirit.

I inherited my belief systems and didn't question whether I embraced their messages which, therefore, hindered my spiritual growth. My mind told me I couldn't question these beliefs and I didn't. I continued these patterns not because they were working but because they were familiar and comfortable. Testing new waters took me out of my comfort zone. It was only when I was finally ready to move through the hurt and pain of my past, to design my life and fulfill my hearts desire, that I began the transformation.

I always needed to control every aspect of my life–determining the how and when of everything that happened. I was so sure I could do a better job than God could, that I shut Him out and dove deeper into my mind. I quit hearing the messages that He was trying to provide. I believed God was the core of my life because I was a Christian and went to church on a regular basis. But, He was only in a physical building. I did not experience Him in my heart.

I was so afraid to trust myself and surrender to God that I gave my power to my mind and denied God within me. Transformation for me is like an artichoke. There are layers and layers that you cannot see. Just when you think you have peeled away your hidden agendas, issues and fears, there are more layers to be shed. Fortunately, I had Lynn to help me shed those layers of hurt that had created a false sense of protection and was able to get to the heart.

I was eager to be in spirit and live my life in my heart and not my mind. In order to make this shift I had to listen to the desires of my heart as opposed to my mind's beliefs. I begged God to help me–learning not to deny my connection with Him and love myself through the process. I accepted that there are lessons, both positive and negative, to be learned. Wisdom is gained through failure and it is also through wisdom that we learn to handle our successes. Surrendering my mind to God allows me to know my truth.

It took me a long time to see the spirit in me that I allowed others to see. I loved my friends, family and strangers unconditionally, but I had a different set of rules for myself. I was to be perfect and it was unacceptable to have failures. I believed everything was my fault and I gave up my very being to be accepted by others. Then, once I gave up my self-respect and spirit for another, they didn't like who I became.

The light went on. Living this human experience is about being who I am–respecting myself and not denying God in me for anyone. I am a gift from God–a gift to be honored. I have to first honor my desires and truths before people will honor me just as I am. I no longer have to be perfect in order to speak my truth. God is always with me, even if others do not agree or like who I am.

What does this transformation mean to me? When anything happens or I receive messages, I ask for God's guidance – meaning that I start with Spirit. If it is through Spirit that the message comes, I am at peace and follow through with the desires of God for

I know that we are one and these are my true desires. If I begin to get cloudy and start analyzing, I know that the message comes from my mind and, once again, surrender it up to God.

Is life perfect now that I have experienced this transformation? It is not as my mind had previously defined perfection. I am at peace with my life and am grateful for the comfort of God in it. Loving myself unconditionally will give me freedom, both spiritually and personally, and this is what I intend for myself.

I am now attending a church of a different faith, not because the faith of my childhood is wrong, but because this is where I hear my truth. I heard this and found it very powerful. "Love should be a free gift from God and others."

I thank God for my gifts. I am a planner, but I now know that God is a much better planner than I am and I trust my life to Him.

Patti

15

Creating Your Dreams

It is imperative to understand that we create our own reality, be it a pleasant or not so pleasant experience. God gives us the ability to create the circumstances that our higher consciousness feels is needed for our highest level of growth. So, often we find ourselves in situations or circumstances that we believe are beyond our control–convincing ourselves that we aren't responsible for being in the midst of what we don't want.

People who continue to believe that someone or something outside of themselves are creating their environment, are, in essence, saying that they are victims of something greater than God. There is nothing greater than God. Once we truly know and embrace the fact that we are co-creators with Him, we can see the inaccuracies in our previous beliefs. I have come to recognize that knowing this concept is not enough and Michael makes sure I experience that which I teach.

Manifesting my desires has never been too much of a problem. However, recognizing I deserved what I manifested is another story. When Kevin and I were first married, we knew that we wanted a house of our own and so purchased one that was only 900 sq. ft. At 21, I became pregnant and knew the home we were living in was much too small to raise a family. So, we purchased a larger one that had 2,000 sq. ft. I knew immediately it was the home of my dreams and that I would raise a family and grow old here.

Our house was quite run down and needed a complete overhaul – a task I embraced wholeheart-edly. We painted, tore up counters, tiled and re-carpeted floors, added a weight room and landscaped the backyard and pool area. I chose, with great care, the interior furnishings and decorations. It was my haven up until that fateful night when I walked in on my husband, his friend and their drugs.

You would think I would have kept my home after all the love, time and energy I had put into it– not to mention the stability it provided for my children. I didn't. We had bought the house from Kevin's parents and although I was told the chances of my being able to stay in it were good, I didn't feel I could do that to Kevin since it once belonged to his family. I signed over the house to Kevin and rented a house for the kids and myself.

A month into my second marriage, Jeff and I purchased a house. Previous to this, we spoke with a real estate agent describing what we wanted and the price we were able to pay. What we were shown in our price range came to no where near what I knew my home was to look like. I knew not to settle and that the home I saw us living in was just on the horizon. Mind you, at this time my concept of Archangel Michael as my guide was purely gut instinct. Also, the concept of being co-creators with God ran more along the lines of "pure luck" bordering on "maybe there's something more to this than just pure luck."

After seeing yet another house and feeling the seeds of doubts starting to creep in, I drove by an intersection with a canopy on the corner and a real estate agent showing HUD Home listings. I pulled in and, much to my delight, spoke with a woman who was as committed to my dream home as I. She had no limitations, just possibilities. Days later she called with some listings for me to look over and when we pulled up to the third house, I knew we'd found it.

At this time, Jeff and I had not yet been pre-qualified. We were told that, if we could get qualified and approved within two weeks, we could get $900.00 of our money back and, if within three weeks, we could get $600.00 back. The Realtor was shooting for three weeks. I was shooting for two. We had our loan and were moved in within two weeks, much to the awe of just about everyone, including Jeff, who, if truth be told, didn't want to buy a house in the first place because of his financial fears. Another masterful link provided by Michael? Absolutely. Did I know it was Michael? No.

While living in this new house, I was effortlessly manifesting all my heart desired. I created our home, Jeff's bronco (that he always wanted) and my dream car, a Jaguar. I say I created them because, although Jeff wanted these things, he never actively pursued anything except the burden of how much all of this was going to cost us and how much overtime or side jobs he would need to provide it.

Jeff has a difficult time believing that you can create whatever you want. If, by some stroke of genius, you *do* create it, then it is a struggle to keep it. I, on the other hand, held the belief that it doesn't *have* to be a struggle. Yet, I had a core belief that I didn't *deserve* it without one. This would have been an ideal time to realize my co-creation was with God and not with Jeff.

Needless to say, we found ourselves at opposite ends of the spectrum trying to hold on to our beliefs until finally succumbing and buying into our logic. We sold the Bronco because we couldn't afford it. We sold the Jaguar because it kept breaking down and we sold the house before the inevitable foreclosure.

It was, at that time, that our marriage was also breaking down. My heart's desire for the life that I knew existed and Jeff's reality of life didn't support each other and we split up for 5 months. The kids and I moved in with my parents and Jeff moved in with friends. Did we actually make an income that supported our creations? Yes. Did we have the faith and belief in our co-creation with God? No.

Jeff and I reconciled and we moved our family into a two-bedroom apartment. Our life together seemed to be on the mend. Neither of us really wanted to move into the confines of apartment life after having a roomy house with a big backyard and a pool. However, we were cleaning up our financial upsets and knew we would have to, meanwhile, bide our time before buying another house.

The fact that my sister and her children lived in a house about a half a mile away made the transition a lot smoother. This allowed my boys to ride their bikes or roller blades to her house at any time.

In the meantime, Jeff encouraged me to do my intuitive counseling out of our apartment – even coming up with ideas that would help build my business. I was elated to finally have his support to pursue my dream career and things were looking up.

We lived in our apartment for approximately nine months and needed to decide whether we were going to sign another lease. It was about this time that Lisa and her family were moving into a new rental house up north and we were helping her move. I walked into the house and Marley, then two years old, told me to follow her because she wanted to show me Uncle Jeffy's and my bedroom. I told her that this wasn't our house, but her house. Yet, moments earlier I had been thinking how I wished another rental like this one would come up in the neighborhood.

Two months later when we absolutely had to make a decision regarding another lease, the house next door to Lisa, and closely identical to hers, came up for rent. I was ecstatic. I loved the house she was living in and to be right next door was a dream come true. Well, at least it was for Lisa and I. Our husbands, on the other hand, were less than thrilled. Yet, being the good sports that they are and seeing that we spend most everyday together anyway, they consented.

Naturally, once I moved into the house, my

first reaction was that it wasn't as wonderful as I had thought it would be and that I had made a mistake. Again, I didn't have to struggle to create my dream so, instead of acknowledging my belief in being undeserving of all the good God and I create, I became disillusioned with my creation. Fortunately, I was now starting to acknowledge that God wanted for me all that I wanted for myself. I could then step into loving and creating a wonderful environment in which to live.

Creativity doesn't stop when you achieve your goal. As with breathing, you don't stop just because you've taken one breath. You continue with the next, and the next and the next. I was given the opportunity to observe my alignment with God and how far I'd progressed in staying centered in my creativity.

After we sold the Jaguar, I bought a Taurus, which is not a bad car. Yet, it was not the car I desired. Jeff at the time was driving a work truck and, thus, didn't need to worry about having two cars. We completed a program that consolidated all our loans and were finally free and clear of all debts. The Taurus was beginning to breakdown frequently which was a sure sign, letting us know, that it was time to allow it to move on. It was during this that friends offered to sell us their 1992 Chevy step-side truck. We bought it and sold the Taurus.

A few months later, Jeff was offered a fabricating job (his dream job) with more pay but had to give up the work truck. It was now time to become a two car family again. For months, I kept asking myself what kind of vehicle I wanted, an Expedition or a Suburban? Just when I thought I knew for sure that I wanted an Expedition, I couldn't decide on what color. Then, when I would decide on a color, I'd want a Suburban.

This insane behavior went on for quite a while. Finally, I got the message to go to the dealerships and see what was out there. Jeff and I got in the car and he asked me if I got a message as to where to go? The fact that Jeff even asked if I had gotten a message, was music to my ears and we joked about it. I told him we needed to go to a nearby dealership. The vehicle we were going to buy was there.

When we got there, neither an Expedition nor Suburban could be seen on the lot. What *was* on the lot, clear as day and as though it was the only one there, was a blue Ford F150, the truck of Jeff's dreams! Right then and there we knew it wasn't my vehicle we were there to purchase, but his! Jeff was extremely confronted by getting the truck of his dreams. Finances again being his limitation, he began looking at little Ford Rangers. They were very nice. However, it was not Jeff's dream truck.

I got the message, loud and clear, that we were not going to settle for less than his dream. This of course was very confronting to me as I thought I was the one getting my dream vehicle. Yet, Michael had, at one point, told me that transportation was Jeff's department and my message now was to "wait for it." After remembering Michael's words, my frustration dissipated and I was able to persuade Jeff into taking a leap of faith. We brought home a new truck.

Once we brought the new truck home, Jeff decided he didn't want to put on all the miles that driving to and from his work would surely do. So, we switched vehicles with myself now driving his dream truck. This worked for awhile until I realized I still didn't have *my* heart's desire and Jeff was, in essence, proving to himself, or at least I knew it as this, that you can't have what you want. He was working harder than ever and I was driving his dream truck.

One afternoon while cleaning the house, Michael told me to call the credit union and get a pre-approved loan for the Suburban that I now knew I desired. My response as usual was, "Are you crazy, Michael?"

I began the inner dialogue asking, "Do you realize my credit is not so good?" Our credit, although cleared, hadn't been so for very long and we had already bought the F150. Michael said it wouldn't be a problem, "just call."

I called reluctantly not wanting to hear the credit union refuse me. They took my information and told me they would call me back in a few hours with a response. I went about my business as usual. Then, after finishing a session, I checked my messages and found the credit union had, indeed, called back.

As Michael had promised, they did in fact have an approval for me to buy a Suburban. All I had to do was simply call them with the details when I found the one I wanted. I was shocked! You would think, by this time, that Id take it all in stride – the way God works in my life. However, it is just the opposite. It's true that I am more confident in following through with his requests. Yet, I'm still in awe each time I receive confirmation of Michael and God's presence in my life.

Now that I was pre-approved, I had to find the vehicle. I called my dad and he recommended I call his friend who's an auto wholesaler. I made the call to Mick and told him what I was looking for and the amount. He voiced his concern at being able to find one for that amount but would keep his eye open. Michael told me to call the credit union and ask for a higher approval amount. Again, I was gifted with a yes.

When Mick called me telling me he had found

the Suburban I was looking for at the price of my original pre-approval, I knew that I was just being tested on my willingness to move forward in the face of my fears. Mick then asked me what color Suburban I wanted and when I said that it didn't really matter, he said, "okay, what is the only color you don't want it in?"

Since Jeff loathes the color green, I said, "green." Dead silence followed. He replied, "Then, this isn't the Suburban for you." Yes, the Suburban was green. Now, it was my turn to act. I called Jeff and told him that we, indeed, found a vehicle for the original amount and the only drawback was that it was green. Simultaneously, Jeff and I both understood that it didn't matter what color it was and, whether Jeff liked it or not, it was my vehicle.

I called Mick back, told him I wanted the Suburban and that I would be over with the check. Mick asked whether I wanted to come by to see it and drive it before I committed to the bank and got the check. Much to his surprise, I said, "No, I knew it was my truck." I went to the bank, picked up the check and went to get my new Suburban sight unseen. Don't get me wrong I had minor butterflies in my stomach wondering what exactly I was buying. But, the moment I drove down the street and saw that beautiful bluish-green metallic vehicle, I knew everything else would proceed without a glitch. I left there driving the most beautiful suburban I could imagine.

My point in describing the details of these experiences, is to show how much people stay in their logic, fretting over minute, seemingly inconsequential things that, very often, have unsettling consequences to their peace of mind.

Purchasing our new home was a bit more challenging. Michael gave me the date of June 17, 2000 saying that this was the date I would be moving into my new home. Again, this was impossible for all the logical reasons with finances being at the top of the list. Jeff was adamant about not buying a house because we were struggling to meet our bills as it was. Although my business was steadily growing, my finances were not as steady as they were when we bought our first home. I knew to follow Michael's messages, yet, questioned my sanity at doing so in the face of Jeff's less than optimistic outlook.

Michael continued to move me forward in the procedures of what needed to be done to start the process. Meanwhile, I dealt with the reactions of the many people who were truly concerned as to how we were going to do this. I felt insecure and sometimes downright ridiculous telling them that I was being guided and that now was the time to buy. However, Michael continued to provide everything for me as long as I followed his guidance which, many times, I did not want to do. At that point, we went about getting pre-qualified for a house. Amazingly, this was not as difficult as I had anticipated and the search for our new home was on.

I contacted Patti, a friend and Realtor, and looked at house-after-house. Yet, every time she found one that fit the needs of our family and my business, invariably the asking price would be too much or they had already accepted another bid. Having succumbed to my logical mind, I thought that Patti would surely either give up or want to kill me. After about a week of continuous mind chatter, such as, "What house is the right house," "how am I going to do this?" or "Jeff is being confronted," etc., I finally snapped out of it and remembered that God was in charge of this process and that all I had to do was surrender to His path. I knew all would be provided.

Everything then fell back into place and we found the most beautiful home that far exceeded what I believed possible. Many more complications occurred as to whether or not we were going to get the house by the seventeenth, as I had been told.

However, Michael kept reassuring me that this was an accurate message and to hold tight to the truth. Whenever I doubted what I knew, my wonderful sister would ask, over and over again, "What is the date?" making me repeat it to her so as not to lose sight of the truth.

By this time, the lender assured us that a contract could be written up so that we did not have to come up with a down payment. Not true. Three weeks before closing, they now told us how much money down was needed and, frankly, we didn't have it. I got the message through my father to approach my uncle with the possibility of loaning us the money. I thought, "Why do I have to do this?"

I don't like asking for help and, though I love my uncle, he wasn't known for his generosity with money, especially in the amount I needed. After I wore myself out with the battle that was taking place inside my head, I finally surrendered. What did I really have to lose? The worst he could do was say, "no" and I would, then, just wait for Michael's next message.

The degree to which my heart opened up, when my uncle readily agreed, was indescribable. I realized then, what a gift it was to each of us – me, in being able to ask for help and he, in the simple act of giving. Smooth sailing from there – right? Wrong.

The original lender, who assured us that all was going well, called up two and one half weeks prior to my June 17th date. The lender said that it was now impossible to go ahead with the loan – some bureaucratic red tape with the financing. Was this ever going to end?

Then, God provided us with a friend whose husband knew of a lender we could try. Miracles do happen when you step beyond judgment and we were introduced to a man who wouldn't take "no" for an answer. His spirit knew no bounds. Our new lender jumped through hoops in tying up the loose ends, never faltering in his mission to get us our home. It wasn't until the last day of closing that he began to have his doubts. We had only two hours to record the documents before the office closed for the weekend. The seventeenth was the next day and we had already given notice to our rental home with no place to go.

My lender told me that he didn't think we were going to be able to get it through until Monday or Tuesday. I asked Michael what to do. His reply was to leave the office, go home and finish packing. He assured me that it was going to be done and I would be moving the next day. Michael was completely accurate. My lender called me an hour and one half later and said, "Congratulations, it's recorded." His other comment was, "Wow, when you know something, you know it!"

Both the lender and I were forever changed from that experience. I have since referred several clients of mine to him. He has told them that there is nothing that can stop him after our experience together. Let me reassure you that he has proven that true. In retrospect, I can see that all the doubts, mind chatter and the questioning of my sanity had to occur for me to really grasp how much Michael is with me and to also see how the Universe works with the other players in this endeavor. I now remember that chaos doesn't always have to represent frenzy in my life. It is possible to find peace within the chaos.

By now I had enough evidence through my vehicle and my home that I was, indeed, creating my dreams. I'd talk to my family about what we wanted our lives to look like. If we were creating our dreams, how would they show up? My son Jacob has wanted a Basset hound for as long as I can remember. We've had dogs and the experiences have been both pleasant and not so pleasant. Jeff wasn't at all pro-dog. I, on the other hand, didn't have a problem with it as long as it was Jacob's dog and not mine.

So, Jacob set out creating his dog. We discussed

that if it was in the highest interest for all, he and God would manifest his desires. But, under no circumstances, were his dad and I to be his source. If he was going to manifest this dog, it wasn't through us buying it for him. He had done previous research on how much it could cost and found it could be upwards of $1300.

Jacob didn't give up. Jeff and I still weren't in agreement about pets and whether Jacob was responsible enough to take care of one. But, then again, Jeff didn't believe in manifesting through your heart's desire to begin with. So, he didn't see anything coming of it. I, on the other hand, knew that we would indeed be getting a dog and got the message, "Summer." As it was only September, I wasn't too worried about Jacob manifesting his dream, at least until next summer.

It was then, in October, that we got a call from my mother saying that a woman at work had three Basset hound puppies that she had found. She was looking to find them homes at no cost. Coincidence? I believe not. What were we going to do? Jeff and I talked it over. Though he wasn't at all for it, he agreed, but only after setting boundaries as to where the dog could be in the house and where it could not.

We didn't tell Jacob, as we wanted it to be a

surprise. We were going to pick the dog up on Friday night and have it here waiting for him when he got home. That Thursday, out of the blue, Jacob informed us that he was getting a dog the next day. Knowing there was no way he could possibly know how impressed I was with his connection to his guide, I, of course, was questioning mine since I had clearly gotten the message "summer."

We brought the dog home and when Jacob walked into his room, our family plus my niece and nephew sang, "Happy Dog Day To You" to the tune of "Happy Birthday." Jake was elated with a smile brighter than I had seen in a long while. I asked him what he was going to name her and he told us that there was a girl named "Summer" on Baywatch that he really liked. That's how his dog, "Summer," came to be. Obviously, my message was accurate. It was my interpretation of the message that was off.

Life should have been bliss, but something was missing. Jeff and I seemed to be drifting apart in spite of all that we had achieved. We had become mechanical in our interactions and we both knew it. After several months, Jeff moved out and the boys and I remained in the house.

Michael told me that we would be divorcing. Our time together had run its course. My judgments came rushing at me full force. How could Michael do this to me? Why hadn't he told me when we married in the first place that it would only last seven years? I told Michael if I had known it wasn't going to be for a lifetime I wouldn't have married in the first place.

That was precisely why I wasn't told. My sons needed Jeff for their father. They needed a place to belong along with the opportunity to take Jeff's last name as their own. I questioned why, when almost three years to the day after we had separated for the first time and had gotten back together, we were to only separate again. I was told that the boys had not, at that time, embraced their need for having the name Ferguson–as to why they wanted it and keep it as their own. Even now, with Jeff and I in the process of divorcing, the boys continue to use his name and are acknowledging their desire to legally have it changed in the future.

I found myself again faced with uncertainty in regards to my future. How in the world was I going to manage hefty house and car payments and take care of utilities? My business was going well, but not, as yet, to the level needed to maintain this lifestyle. Michael told me that I was to keep my house and vehicle, at least until the boys were finished with school. This was another eight months away and Jeff was not at all in favor of this plan. He wanted to sell the house and have the boys and myself get an apartment near the school.

I knew Michael's message was for the highest good of all concerned – for the boys' stability and for us, as parents, in following through at providing necessities, even in the face of discord. The only problem was that Jeff refused to help out with the mortgage. I had asked him to pay half until June and I would pay the other half. Keeping the house and Suburban was a huge undertaking and my mind was having a very difficult time seeing how this was going to transpire. Jeff's mind was having the same difficulties. However, I had Michael's message and knew I must follow through as I had done many times before. I was determined.

Obviously, by having private sessions out of my home, people were bound to know that Jeff and I were no longer living together. It's not that I was ashamed of the choice he and I had made. We were both clear it was the path we needed to take. It was, instead, the judgment that I had placed upon myself in being this "spiritual" counselor who was going through a second divorce. How would that look to people? How did it look to me? What would people say when I would have to leave my home because I couldn't pay the mortgage?

I had helped so many people overcome their financial challenges, even helping them move on to great success. Here I was holding on to messages that only I could hear? I stayed centered and was touched at the support I received. I've always been great at defending and supporting the messages I get for other people in relation to their dreams. It was a huge wake-up call when I realized how hard it was for me to accept people supporting my dreams. When I accepted the love and support given to me by family, friends and clients, my quest for self-acceptance began.

Thankfully, after seeing a lawyer, Jeff was convinced that what I was asking for was much less than what the lawyer informed him I would be entitled to in the divorce. I also knew that he was feeling like he needed to finish his part in helping me to get current on the mortgage that was now overdue by a few months. He came up with half. I had to come up with the rest.

How I was going to do that was beyond my own comprehension. I simply "knew" to stay centered and the message of what to do would be there. I was very fortunate to have my sister, parents and very close friend Holly, who, along with her husband Carlos had helped me financially many times before, hold the space for me so as not to lose sight of the outcome needed to produce this feat. They were ruthless! Whenever I would falter, they were there to help me regain my commitment.

The first message I received was to call a relative and ask if she could loan me some money. I needed enough to get through the next few months and relieve the pressure in order to finish writing this book. After a few days, I received a response that I was not wanting to hear. She was heartbroken. The last thing she wanted to do was disappoint me. However, she was unable to help me at this time. I couldn't understand at the time why Michael would have me ask her if the answer was going to be no. His answer was, "We have many different avenues in which things can manifest. However, free will to choose is always a factor."

The next message came quickly on the heels of my previously discouraging "no" through a conversation with my sister. Mother Mary had guided her to have me call an old friend from the past which also happened to be a heartfelt relationship of hers that had "gone south." The difficulty, not to mention the humiliation I was feeling at the time, was enormous. I was feeling as though I had to grovel to save my house and vehicle.

However, this was not the case. Michael was

allowing me to stand in the confidence of my work and in my commitment to myself, to my sons and the dream I *knew* to be real, which was writing this book. Manifesting this book was my response to a request Spirit had made of me. However, at the time, I was not quite seeing it that way. By this time, making another phone call seemed like a huge request, especially given the terms in which my sister had left her relationship.

With courage I picked up the phone and called him without even knowing I had dialed nor asked for him. To my amazement and later, delight, Michael spoke flawlessly through me as he has in every session that I have ever had. Through Michael, I gave every detail of my circumstance and why it was advantageous for him to support me and my work. Included, also, was the information regarding my publisher. The conversation was very heartfelt, but business-like, and he said he would get back to me regarding his decision.

Waiting for his phone call was a most nerve racking experience. I went from one extreme to the other. Not knowing I had a deadline in which I needed to pay my past due mortgage, he took an entire week to notify me of his decision. I was reassured by Lisa, Holly, Carlos, Michael and my mother that everything was going to work out perfectly. I *knew* the message to call him was accurate. However, I also *knew* the message to call my relative was accurate. Here, I was again *knowing* that free will is a factor from which you cannot get away and that when someone falls into logic or fear, it changes everything.

Then, his call came and the answer was, "no!" I couldn't believe my ears. I was devastated. Twice I had humbled myself and swallowed my pride, which is what was truly needed to move me through this. He said he had every faith in me and my work. However, he had been burned too many times lending money to people he cared for and was unwilling – there's that free will creeping in – to get burned again. He knew I would never intentionally burn him. However, he was not willing to have tension between us.

Meanwhile, two very dear friends, Jack and Pam, approached me with a proposition that they had given me years ago when I first began my business. The original offer was to give me money to help get my foundation started. I declined, at that time, because it didn't feel right. I did not yet have my foundation formulated and nothing substantial to put the money toward.

However, now was a different story. I needed money to help get the book printed. Their offer was a gift I couldn't refuse and I accepted it with great appreciation and gratitude. I am truly blessed to have friends and clients that support who I am, enough for them to step up and help me in a huge time of need. Although the gift of being able to start the process on the book was a blessing indeed, I still found myself in the midst of possible foreclosure.

This is when my sister stepped in. She got another message from Mother Mary that her friend was indeed the catalyst for making things happen and not to give up even though his answer had been "no." She went right back to the drawing board and called. If my calling him took enormous courage, Lisa doing so was nothing short of miraculous.

Lisa had to give up her conversations of unworthiness in failing both herself and her friend. They had shared a great love and were on the brink of marriage when all of Lisa's fears arose to sabotage everything that they had worked so hard to overcome. Although she knew, in her heart, that they still had love for one another, she didn't know whether he could look past the hurt that her "betrayal" had caused him. Fortunately, for the three of us, he could and did. My financial dilemma was resolved. Lisa's fears were put to rest and our friend's heart opened once again. These were all gifts that could only have been given through Spirit.

16
The Final Step

The message that my marriage was at an end came as a huge surprise to me. I was unaware of how judgmental I was being about the state my marriage had deteriorated to and had chosen to ignore the final signs. I had been doing this work for nearly four years, building it from scratch through word of mouth. Though it had become successful in it's own right, the strain of my finances were clearly showing me that there was still something holding me back from embracing all of myself and my truth.

My husband had been supportive even though he was continuously confronted by the work that I was doing. As much as he loved the person, Lynn, he still could not come to grips with the fact that I communicated with Archangel Michael and had such faith in his messages that I followed them implicitly and without question.

To Jeff's credit, he had been extremely patient with the process it took for me to build my clientele. His worry came from carrying the financial burden and his fears that, although the business was starting to do well, it wasn't expanding quickly or profitably enough for us to maintain our lifestyle. Though we were both working very hard, his negative feelings regarding my work made it difficult for me to prosper knowing that all he wanted was for me to make money.

It's ironic that when Jeff and I first began dating, money didn't hold the power he now gave it in his life. He drove what he called his "Galactic Cruiser" (a beat up old Buick) and was happy doing so. I can see that in my desires for a nice home and vehicles, and Jeff's wanting to provide these for us, that I had a part to play in his consciousness shifting from being financially laid-back to money-driven.

In my eyes, I do this work because I love doing it. Money is a bi-product of that love with financial success manifesting out of that love. Jeff's experience of work lies in his interest to pay bills and get ahead so that he can enjoy life with less struggle. I understood his point. However, it was a catch 22 for me. Understand, I wanted to pay our bills as much as he did. It was that our methods of getting there differed and we couldn't agree to disagree and come up with a resolution that would be a compromise for both our standards.

My experience of putting my heart first and allowing the abundance to flow was too "out of touch with reality" for his logical approach. It was simply not working for us. I was falling into my logical mind every time I dealt with Jeff regarding my work and what I felt guided to do.

If I make this work about money, I lose the intent my heart has for helping those in need, whether or not they have the financial means to pay my fee. That would make it only a job instead of the dream of my heart. I knew, through Michael, that I would do very well financially, but it was not my first intention.

I was not able to communicate this to Jeff, especially with his lack of support, which was now coming through in belittling comments or even more so in the sarcastic tone in which he said them. He would say, "Why don't we ask Archangel Michael what we should do?" or "Maybe Michael will give you some money."

One day, in particular, I was feeling the pull, more than usual, to make money. I felt I was being made to go against my own heart. It felt shameful to fall into Jeff's logical reasons for why I should promote my business. After all, Michael has always led me to the path that would be in my best interest. He even led me in how to promote myself, which I knew to be through word-of-mouth, and, now, in writing this book. Doing it the way Jeff wanted, felt horrible.

On one particular morning, Joy, a very dear friend of mine, was visiting from out of town. Jeff and I at this time were still married and hadn't yet made the final decision to separate. Joy and I were discussing my financial situation in all its bleakness. We were working on finding the deep issue underneath my block, when her partner, who has also become a dear friend over the years, called.

At the time, he said something that didn't make any sense to me at all. He asked me if I had an old boyfriend named Anthony. I thought back and said "no". He said he needed to relay a message he'd received that didn't seem to make sense. He said there was something incomplete with this old boyfriend named Anthony and myself. Not wanting to hinder my friend's helpful intuitive message, I simply replied, "Huh, I don't know, maybe it's an old boyfriends middle name or something!" We dropped the subject and moved on to discuss other issues.

Later that afternoon, as Joy and I were going to dinner, we were driving past an old boyfriend's house that I dated 19 years ago. I mentioned to her that while we were dating, he and his best friend had gotten into a car accident and his best friend had died. I wondered how he was doing now in his life as his friend's death had really taken a toll on him and we had broken up shortly afterward.

Five days later, while attending a lecture during "Spirit Week" at church, I was mesmerized by the guest minister who was speaking and his fiancée who is an incredible spiritual singer. The connection these two people shared was amazing. You could feel Spirit connecting their hearts as they shared themselves with the audience. The deep emotion I felt was beyond explanation and I remember thinking to myself, "I'm going to have that."

I had been waiting at least three years now for Jeff and I to regain the once very heartfelt connection we had during our first years of marriage. I was living in my connection to Michael and God, believing that was enough to sustain my heart.

At the same time, I was living life and marriage logically with Jeff, just as he was living in his logical mind shutting his heart off to me completely. I didn't realize until that very moment sitting in the audience watching these two beautiful souls share their hearts so openly, that I didn't know how much I was living in my logical mind within my marriage.

I missed the spiritual partnership Jeff and I used to share and remembered our relationship of many years prior when both of our hearts were open to each other. I walked out of the church feeling empty and lost. I had been holding onto a marriage without a spiritual connection because I loved him and didn't want to go through a divorce or put my kids through the trauma of letting go again. Loving him outside the heart was simply not enough any longer. Until that night, I was content to wait, thinking that time would change where we had come to in our marriage, returning us to where we had started.

I know now that I was living logically and this was part of the reason I would not allow my finances to flow. I had spiritual partnerships in all areas in my life with family, friends, and clients. I worked very hard in releasing relationships with those who were not mutually willing to share their hearts with me, including clients unwilling to open their hearts. Some clients were only willing to play the games of the mind. I often found myself referring them to other sources or waiting until they were open before engaging in conversation.

My husband had been unwilling for a long time and I was frightened to let the marriage go for all the logical reasons. We got along fine and seemed to have a very normal life, by societies' standards, but our hearts were no longer connected, nor did they wish to be.

Two days after my experience in the church that had clarified what I longed for in a spiritual partnership, my father called. He asked if I had been thinking about anyone. I laughed and said, "I think of lots of people, why?" Dad knows that many times all I do is think of someone and they call. It's amazing how God links people up.

My dad said that a guy named Mike called for me and had left his number asking that I call him back. It is important to note that Lisa and I have moved many times. Our parents, on the other hand, have had the same telephone number and address for the past 24 years. I was shocked. This was the old boyfriend's house I had driven past with Joy just one week prior. I wondered if maybe he had heard about the work I was doing and wanted to see if I could help him reconnect with his friend that had passed away so many years earlier.

I called him. To my surprise, he hadn't any idea what I did for a living. In fact, he wasn't sure why he was looking me up after so many years. He said that he simply felt an overwhelming urge to call me. We talked for some time catching up on the last 19 years and, then, I began telling him of my work with Archangel Michael. He was very interested. In fact, he had had many of the same experiences that I had had.

However, he chose to shut his connection off many years earlier and, due to his fear, worked very hard at not opening the door because it scared him. He is a hearing-based person, and like many hearing-based intuits that don't understand what they are hearing, they use devices to shut it down, such as alcohol or drugs. It can be very disturbing to hear Spirit if you do not understand that it is indeed Spirit you are hearing.

Michael and I knew that there was a reason we were brought together after so many years. He was going through a very tough time, questioning what his purpose was in life and without a doubt Archangel Michael had directed this introduction knowing I could help him to answer that question.

Michael, not to be confused with Archangel Michael, is a very gifted intuit that doesn't understand his gift as a "gift." Archangel Michael also guides Michael. Therefore, we share many of the same challenges in our lives, which made it comfortable, from the beginning, for Michael to trust that I could help him. I, however, was not sure why he was brought into my life. Then, one day when I was doing some healing work with him, out of the blue, he says to me, "You know my real name is Anthony." When he said this, I thought, "Why is he telling me this?"

Two days later, at 6:00 a.m., and out of a deep sleep, I sat straight up out of bed. Archangel Michael was reminding me of the conversation regarding an old boyfriend named Anthony and of something being incomplete between us. In all these years, I never knew his first name was Anthony. He has always gone by Mike or Michael.

The boys in his family go by their middle names instead of their first. The connection started to sink in. I was beginning to understand what was incomplete with us. Until I put everything together, I always wondered why Archangel Michael had brought Michael back into my life.

Metaphorically speaking, there are times in our lives when the elevator doors begin to shut and we can put our hand between them to stop them once, twice, or even three times until, finally, the doors just shut. You are either, then, on the inside moving to the next floor or you remain on the outside waiting for the next elevator to come. Watching the minister and his fiancée was my message that it was time. I needed to move to the next level NOW! Archangel Michael had brought Michael to help me awaken my heart once again.

Unfortunately, this was my biggest fear. Letting go of my marriage was an obstacle with which I did not want to deal. Having been brought up in a Catholic environment, I had decided years ago that divorce was not an option. I was judging myself enormously and allowed my mind chatter to convince me that if I continued to follow my heart all would work out between Jeff and me.

My mind was not going to allow me to justify letting go of this marriage as it had in my first. Afterall, there was no abuse, either verbal or physical, nor was there any adultery. My mind was racing with all the reasons why you hold onto a marriage that looks, by all accounts, wonderful on the outside, yet has no heart.

What I failed to see was that my logical mind had taken over and I was being dogmatic about keeping my marriage together out of beliefs that were not mine. I knew that the love I was experiencing with Jeff was of my mind; the stability and safety we had established through physically being together. Yet, I also knew the emptiness of my heart when sitting next to him, sharing space with him and feeling completely isolated and alone–void of the warmth of our hearts.

I knew a change had to be made and I asked Jeff if he was willing to do anything to transform our situation. His response was, "We see things too differently." That was the truth! Our paths had gone in different directions. To stay together, each of us would have had to consciously go against our own truths to make it work – something we had been doing unconsciously for years that now was becoming ugly.

Jeff's belittling remarks directed toward me such as calling "coincidences" what I refer to as "miracles of God," were no longer acceptable. I believe in God, he does not. I believe in miracles, he in coincidences. This is perfectly workable if you're both willing to accept and respect the other's belief. However, as I said before, NO ONE HAS THE RIGHT TO TELL YOU YOUR EXPERIENCE OF GOD IS WRONG AND YOU DO NOT HAVE THAT RIGHT EITHER.

Letting go was the only way we could see to salvage the love we had built together in our six and a half years of marriage. We let go with the intention of loving one another and our children. We are committed to providing our children with the love and support they have come to know in us as parents.

I had experienced such a tumultuous divorce the first time around that creating and living into this intention for our family was foreign ground. I must say that our family's commitment to peace is strong and though many people want to judge our family by placing boundaries on what a "normal" happy family looks like, our experience is that when you follow the truth of your heart there will always be peace, love and happiness.

Many people have told me that staying married is the most important thing, even when there is no heartfelt spiritual connection. I disagree. My experience is that you cannot find safety and stability in this world until you look within and allow all of your needs to be met by God. You will always fall short of any hope of true peace until this has been accomplished.

Jesus told us to be *in the world but not of it.* We teach our children to do just the opposite. We teach them conceptually that our home, school, all that is found outside and, in many cases, marriage is where we find stability and safety. This is why we find that often when our so-called safety is changed or altered, such as moving to a different home, school or job, etc., we suffer great anxieties and fear.

This is not because disruption is wrong, but because we have taught them to be reliant upon the world and it's stability instead of developing our ability to remain centered with God in any circumstance. This is a teaching of Michael's to which I have to constantly stay true. Jacob, Adam and I have become stronger for these very circumstances, having to rely upon our connection to God much more fully due to "our world" changing so many different times.

It is that false sense of security that lies outside of us which keeps us living in the same houses, neighborhoods and schools. It is the same cycle we have been in our entire lives – complaining, yet, unable to do anything about it. Some parents will stay in a marriage when the undercurrents of animosity, fear, and even false pleasantries or numbness, to name a few, are so strong that they are destructive to both themselves and their children. We think we're protecting ourselves and our children by keeping our outside world consistent which only maintains an illusion of security.

This is not to say that routine and structure don't have their place. I merely suggest that when you align yourself with God, you will experience peace, safety and security in all people and things, no matter what physical reality dictates.

Eventually, no matter how safe we try to remain cocooned in our own little world, traumatic events occur that change our perspective such as divorce, accidents, deaths or crimes. The list goes on. What I know is that we will all, including our children, find God within us during these disruptive times.

My job as a parent is very simple! I acknowledge that I am a human being making daily errors, learning and growing and that my children's source is within themselves and not in me. I must also direct them at all times back to their heart where the Source truly is. Had Jacob not gone to his heart where his desire for a dog truly resided, he would not yet have Summer. For, as I mentioned, if he would have looked at his mother, Lynn, as his source, the desire for a dog at this time would not have manifested.

I am concluding this book with a blessing that all of you consistently follow your heart and live your truth boldly. God in you is the greatest gift you can give yourself in this world! Never deny your truth, whether it is through communicating with Archangel Michael, as it is for me, or through being a teacher, singer, actor, business developer, homemaker or any truth that lays in your heart to be in order that you may fully experience this world.

The final step is not that I have *stepped* beyond judgment, only that I am committed to my truth and living my life's journey in the process of always *stepping* beyond judgment. Every day I am challenged with the judgments of my own logical mind, as well as the logical minds of others in the world that will still judge me. Yet, I continue through the love that I receive from God and Archangel Michael. My commitment to them gives me the courage to proceed in life–fully expressing myself. Simply put, the final step is being ME.

In the fourth grade, I had to fill out a paper stating my favorite color, food and various things about myself including answering the question, "What do you want to be when you grow up?" I ran across this paper recently and was astounded by my answer to that last question. In big bold letters I had written, "**ME!**" I am pleased to say I have achieved my heart's desire!

Authors Note:

Some names have been changed throughout this book
to protect the identities of those involved.